A little course in...

Preserving

A little course in...

Preserving

LONDON, NEW YORK, MUNICH, MELBOURNE, DELHI

Senior Editor Alastair Laing
Project Art Editor Gemma Fletcher
Managing Editor Penny Warren
Managing Art Editor Alison Donovan
Senior Jacket Creative Nicola Powling
Jacket Design Assistant Rosie Levine
Pre-production Producer Sarah Isle
Senior Producers Seyhan Esen, Jen Lockwood
Art Directors Peter Luff, Jane Bull
Publisher Mary Ling

DK India
Editors Vibha Malhotra, Kokila Manchanda
Assistant Art Editors Karan Chaudhary, Tanya Mehrotra
DTP Manager Sunil Sharma
DTP Designers Sourabh Challariya, Rajesh Singh Adhikari

Tall Tree Ltd
Editor Joe Fullman
Designer Jonathan Vipond

Written by Susannah Steel,
with additional recipes by Amanda Wright

First published in Great Britain in 2013 by
Dorling Kindersley Limited, 80 Strand, London WC2R 0RL
Penguin Group (UK)

2 4 6 8 10 9 7 5 3 1
001–188214–Jan/2013

A CIP catalogue record for this book is available
from the British Library.

ISBN 978 1 4093 6444 3

Printed and bound by Leo Paper Products Ltd, China

Discover more at
www.dk.com

Contents

1
Start Simple

2
Build On It

3
Take It Further

PUBLISHER'S NOTE
The recipes contained in this book have
been created for the ingredients and
techniques indicated. The Publisher is not
responsible for your specific health or
allergy needs that may require supervision.
Nor is the Publisher responsible for any
adverse reactions you may have to the
recipes contained in the book, whether you
follow them as written or modify them to
suit your personal dietary needs or tastes.

Build Your Course

This book divides into broad sections that allow you to build a three-stage course in preserving. All areas are covered, from pickles to potted meats, with recipes that increase in difficulty to develop your skills base and set new challenges as you grow in confidence and experience.

Getting Started

Take your first steps with the preserves in Start Simple, which are easy to master and provide essential foundation skills. In Build On It you will discover many of the classic preserves and, once they are added to your repertoire, you can really call yourself a skilled home preserver. While the recipes in Take It Further feature more unusual and advanced preserving techniques, many with a "wow!" factor that will really stretch your skills and give you a chance to show off.

Clear photographs of every crucial stage demonstrate how to carry out each preserving technique correctly

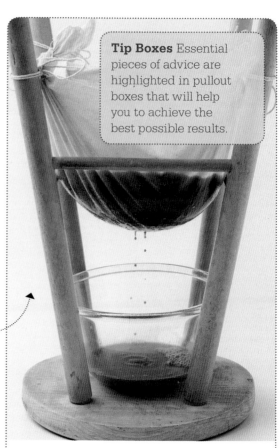

Tip Boxes Essential pieces of advice are highlighted in pullout boxes that will help you to achieve the best possible results.

Recipe information

Symbols for each recipe highlight the amount of preserve you can expect to make, how long it will take to prepare, and its maxiumum shelf life.

These details feature at the start of each recipe

3 large jars

1½ hours plus straining

12 months

How to **Pages**

Each type of preserve is introduced on "How to" pages, which pinpoint the key techniques to understand before tackling a recipe. Here we explain both the "how?" and the "why?", since understanding the reasons for doing something is crucial to getting it right.

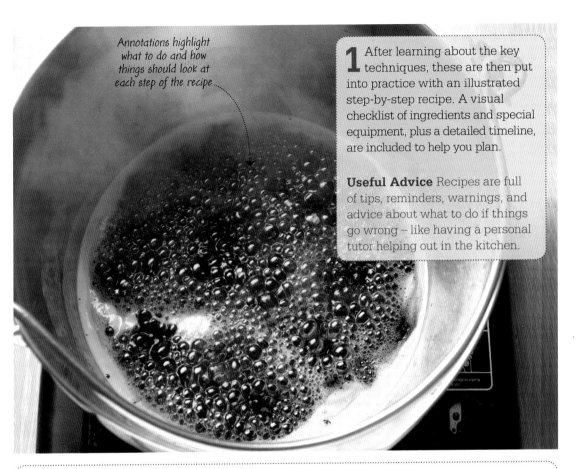

Annotations highlight what to do and how things should look at each step of the recipe...

1 After learning about the key techniques, these are then put into practice with an illustrated step-by-step recipe. A visual checklist of ingredients and special equipment, plus a detailed timeline, are included to help you plan.

Useful Advice Recipes are full of tips, reminders, warnings, and advice about what to do if things go wrong – like having a personal tutor helping out in the kitchen.

How to store

At the end of each practice recipe, you will find further information about how and where to store your preserves, how long to leave them until their flavours mature (if applicable), and how long they will keep and how to store them once opened.

Did anything go wrong?

Perfection can be difficult to achieve at the first attempt and here you will also find common problems anticipated, explanations for what probably went wrong, and advice for how to avoid making the same mistake next time.

Try other fruits, vegetables, and flavour combinations

Suggestions for how to vary the recipe the next time you try it by using different fruits or vegetables, or changing additional flavourings such as herbs and spices, are also provided.

Further tips

And look out for additional nuggets of advice, for example on how to select and prepare the best quality produce or how to successfully adapt a basic recipe when preserving different produce.

Now turn over and start preserving! ▶ ▶ ▶

Essential **Equipment**

MAKING

Much of the equipment used in preserving is not specialist and can be found in most kitchens. For certain techniques, however, you will need specific tools. Here are the essential items that should meet all your preserving needs, and help you produce results of professional quality.

Small ladle
Essential for potting up all kinds of preserves.

Slotted spoon
Useful for poaching fruit and vegetables, or for skimming.

Wooden spoon
Ideal for stirring simmering fruit preserves and chutneys.

Jam (sugar) thermometer
Essential for finding the accurate setting-point temperature.

Hydrometer
Useful for brewing to measure the alcohol content.

Tongs
When heat processing, tongs are essential for removing items from the water.

Wide-mouthed jam funnel
Useful for potting up preserves easily and cleanly.

Long-spouted funnel
Makes easy work of bottling drinks and sauces.

Cheesecloth or calico straining bag
For filtering and straining liquids. Particularly useful when brewing.

Jelly bag
Great for straining fruit pulp to make jellies and cordials.

Muslin cloth
Can be used as a strainer, to wrap meats, or to make spice bags.

Food processor
*Saves time and effort when
mixing, blitzing, mashing, or
pulping fruit and vegetables.*

Large plastic container with drip tray
*Ideal for brining and curing
meats, especially large joints.*

Butter mould
*For easily making
decorative pats of butter.*

Demijohn, airlock, and siphon
*The essential kit for brewing: for storing the
fermenting liquid, sealing, and bottling.*

Stainless steel preserving pan
*Non-reactive, heavy-based, and wide, this specialist pan
is ideal for rapid boiling and making up large quantities.*

STORING

Using the right container can make all the difference in preserving. Whether large or small, functional or decorative, glass, earthenware or freezer-grade plastic, there is a container to suit every preserve. Containers must always be in good condition and sterilized before use (see opposite).

Clear glass bottle
Used with an airtight cork, these are perfect for wines, cider, and cordials.

Ice cube box
For freezing small portions of herbs.

Plastic freezer boxes
Use for freezer jams and for freezing fruit, vegetables, purées, and cooked sauces.

Jam jars
For storing jams, conserves, marmalades, and jellies. Use a new lid, or waxed disc and cellophane cover, every time.

Corks
For stoppering home brews. Ensure they are airtight to prevent oxidization.

Swing stopper bottle
Use for bottling cordials, syrups, and juices.

Ramekin dish
These are the perfect size for potted meats and fish, and for potting up fruit butters, cheese, and jellies.

Specialist preserving jars
Heat-resistant, with non-corrosive lids and replaceable seals, these are specially designed for heat processing (see opposite).

Hygiene and **Food Safety**

Scrupulous hygiene is essential to successful preservation. All equipment and containers must be thoroughly sterilized, and your produce should be of prime quality, kept at the correct temperatures, and consumed within the recommended dates. Any produce showing signs of deterioration should be discarded.

Hygiene Protocol

- Make sure all kitchen surfaces and equipment are completely clean before you start. Remember to use clean cloths and to wash your hands frequently.

- Check that your fridge is clean and set at the correct temperature (4°C/40°F).

- Sterilize all jars, bottles, containers, lids, and equipment that you are using, preferably so that they are ready just before you need them. This ensures that any microbes, which might spoil your preserves, are destroyed.

- Be sure to seal your foods properly before storing. Check on them regularly, use them within date, and throw away any that show signs of deterioration.

- Be extra-careful with meat and fish (raw or cooked). Use the best-quality produce, keep them cold at all times, and separate from other foods. Make sure you use clean equipment at every stage of the process.

Sterilizing Methods

Oven Wash jars, bottles, and lids in hot water, drain, and then dry in a cool oven (140°C/ 275°F/Gas 1) for 15 minutes.
Dishwasher Put jars, bottles, and lids through a hot wash just before use.
Microwave For non-metal jars. Microwave jars with 4 tablespoons of water in each for 2 minutes. Drain, then dry on kitchen paper.
Water bath Put containers in a pan, cover with water, bring slowly to the boil, then turn off the heat. Leave until needed.

Heat Processing

If storing bottled fruits and sauces long-term, they must be heat processed in a water bath. As the water is heated, any air remaining in the container expands and is released. The seal is then tightened, and a vacuum forms when cool. The container is now completely airtight and its contents protected. If successful, the lid should be sealed firmly in place. For full method and processing times, see pp.116–121.

Essential **Ingredients**

SALT

Salt, or sodium chloride, has long been one of our most important natural preservatives. It works by drawing out the moisture in foods, thus preventing the growth of microorganisms. The higher the concentration of salt, particularly in solutions, the more powerful a preservative it becomes. Salt can be used for preserving vegetables, fish, and meat.

Curing salt
A fine salt designed for curing meat.

Rock salt
Coarse, unrefined rock salt is good for general preserving.

SUGAR

When used in high enough concentrations (60% or higher), sugar is as effective a preservative as salt, and works in a similar way, by drawing the moisture out of foods. It is mostly used for preserving fruit, but can also be used with vinegar to preserve fruit and vegetable mixtures, such as chutneys.

Granulated sugar
A refined sugar with coarse granules. Ideal for general sweet preserves.

Caster sugar
Finer than granulated and easily dissolved, it is useful for syrups and cordials.

Soft light brown sugar
The molasses in this sugar can add depth of flavour to chutneys and marmalades.

Jam sugar
Contains added pectin, for use with low-pectin fruits to help them set.

FATS

Although not preserving agents, oils and animal fats have a useful role in preserving. Used to cover already processed foods, they form a seal protecting the produce from airborne microorganisms. Blanched and dried vegetables and potted meats can be protected by fats.

Butter
Butter is clarified and then used to seal potted meats.

Goose fat
Used for sealing potted meats as an alternative to lard.

Olive oil
Its delicious fruity flavour makes it the ideal oil for preserving.

Sunflower oil
An oil with a lighter, more subtle flavour.

VINEGARS

Another important preserving agent of long-standing, vinegar is made by fermenting alcohol to produce acetic acid. Provided its acid content is 5% or higher, vinegar will prevent the growth of most microorganisms, including e-coli, which cause food to deteriorate. It is mostly used to preserve vegetables as pickles, relishes, and sauces, and also oily fish.

Malt vinegar
This strong brown vinegar is suitable for savoury preserves with robust flavours.

Pickling and spirit vinegar
Pickling vinegar can be bought ready-spiced, or home-made from spirit vinegar (see p57).

Red wine vinegar
Fermented from red wine, this vinegar can be used for added colour and flavour.

White wine vinegar
Fermented from white wine, this vinegar has a lighter, more delicate flavour than red.

Cider vinegar
Fermented from cider, this vinegar has a subtle flavour of apples.

LEMONS

Lemons can be invaluable when making jams and jellies. When using fruits with a low-pectin content, adding lemon juice draws out the pectin, helping the mixture to set.

The acid in lemon juice also helps prevent the sugar in sweet preserves from crystallizing.

SPICES AND FLAVOURING

Adding herbs and spices can hugely enhance your preserves. Not only do they add wonderful flavours and aromas, but many can aid digestion and even actively help the preserving process.

Ground spices
Whenever possible, grind whole spices just before use; once ground, they can quickly lose their flavours and aromas.

Herbs
Fresh or dried herbs will enhance the flavours of pickles, relishes, and vegetables in oil. They can also be used to flavour jellies for classic accompaniments to roasted meats.

Whole spices
Whole spices will keep for up to two years in an airtight container. Most often used for flavouring vinegar, they can be left in the jar or tied in a muslin bag and removed before potting (see p.57).

The science of **How Foods Spoil**

Microorganisms such as fungi, yeasts, and bacteria are present in all living things, in the atmosphere, and on the surface of food. In moist, warm, airy, alkaline conditions these microorganisms thrive, causing foods to deteriorate and spoil. Enzymes are organic catalysts present in plant and animal cells that contribute to the rate at which foods spoil.

Enzymes are naturally occurring proteins in food that speed up, or catalyze, the chemical reactions caused by microorganisms that change the appearance, texture, and taste of food. However, enzymes are fragile: they can be destroyed by very high heat or slowed down by very cold temperatures.

Enzymes help convert one set of molecules into different molecules through a chemical reaction

Diagram of enzyme action

Different enzymes are designed to work on or "fit" specific molecules

Enzyme latches on to molecules to catalyze them

Products are released

Enzyme is ready to catalyze further molecules

Bacteria In the right conditions, single-celled bacteria will multiply rapidly and cause food to decay. For example, they can turn warm, unsterilized milk sour in a matter of hours. Some bacteria can also cause food poisoning, so care must always be taken when preserving meat, fish, or vegetables under oil.

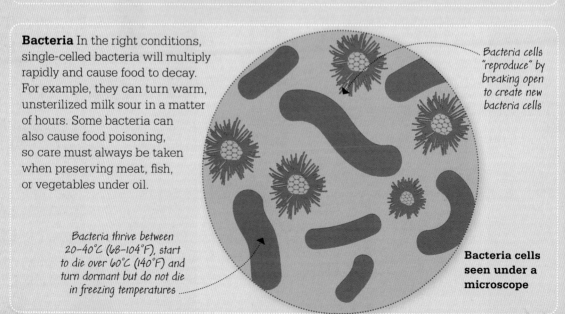

Bacteria cells "reproduce" by breaking open to create new bacteria cells

Bacteria thrive between 20–40°C (68–104°F), start to die over 60°C (140°F) and turn dormant but do not die in freezing temperatures

Bacteria cells seen under a microscope

Moulds are microscopic fungi that live on moist foods in warm, humid conditions. Most are threadlike organisms with roots, or rhizoids, that grow down into a food source, and fruiting bodies that rise up with spores at the tip. The spores, which give a mould its colour, are released when dry to float through the air to form new moulds. While a few moulds are beneficial – in cheesemaking, for example – others will cause foods to rot, and can release harmful toxins.

Sporangium

Germinating spores released into the air

Stalk of fruiting body (sporangiophore)

The mould fungus sends out "runner" roots called stolons that bud to form new "fruits"

Rhizoids anchor the mould, send enzymes to break down the food source, and absorb the nutrients released

Diagram of mould fungus

Yeast Part of the fungi group of organisms, single-celled yeasts prefer warm, moist, slightly acidic environments. Like mould, yeasts secrete enzymes that break down organic matter into nutrients they can absorb. Some yeasts are useful, breaking down, or "fermenting", sugars to produce alcohol and carbon dioxide, which also causes bread to rise. Other yeasts spoil food and cause disease.

A budlike swelling forms on a fully grown yeast cell and separates into a new yeast cell

Yeast cells seen under a microscope

The science of **How To Preserve**

The aim of preserving is to slow down the activity of microorganisms and enzymes or destroy them altogether; they cannot survive in acidic or dry conditions, in high concentrations of salt and sugar, in alcohol, or in high temperatures. A preserve will often employ different techniques, for example jams combine heat with a high concentration of sugar.

Freeze The colder a food is, the slower its rate of deterioration. Bacterial action reduces with refrigeration, while freezing stops it altogether; enzyme activity, however, is only slowed down. Vegetables must be blanched in boiling water first to destroy enzymes and microorganisms, while herbs can be mixed with oil and fruit should be sprinkled with sugar to limit enzyme activity while frozen.

Herbs in water can be frozen in ice cube trays

If food is frozen to -18°C (0°F), microorganisms can't function

Once frozen food is thawed, the enzyme and microorganism activity accelerates again

Freezing herbs

Heat Boiling or blanching food at high temperatures destroys all enzyme activity and almost all microorganisms. The more acidic the food, such as fruit, the more easily microorganisms are destroyed by heat. Boiled preserves must be sealed in airless conditions (e.g. airtight jars) to prolong their shelf life.

Most bacteria will be killed at 100°C (212°F), the boiling point of water

Pot preserves while still hot to maintain the benefits of boiling

Boiling to make fruit preserves

Enzymes start to be destroyed above 60°C (140°F)

Use strong concentrations

Alcohol, acid, and salt and sugar in high concentrations all create environments that prevent the growth of microorganisms or, in the case of alcohol, destroy them completely. Naturally acidic fruit is usually preserved in a concentrated sugar solution or alcohol. Vegetables, which are more alkaline, are preserved in acidic vinegar or a salt solution, or a combination of both.

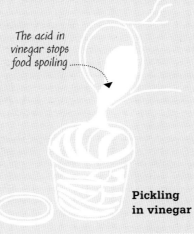

The acid in vinegar stops food spoiling

Pickling in vinegar

Fermenting alcohol

Yeasts can ferment and spoil foods but they can also be harnessed to preserve fruit juices by converting them into an alcoholic concentration.

Exclude air

A seal of fat or oil can prevent any airborne microorganisms coming into contact with food and spoiling it. It also starves aerobic bacteria present in food of oxygen, which it requires to survive and increase. Heat processing jars and bottles of preserves prolongs shelf life by forcing air to escape as steam to leave a sterile vacuum.

Air escapes from partially sealed containers as they are boiled in water

Heating produce also helps destroy harmful organisms

Heat processing bottled produce

Remove moisture

Microorganisms need moisture to grow, and die off in dry conditions. Food can be dried using warm air or an oven, or sealed in a concentrated solution of salt or sugar that draws out moisture by osmosis.

Air-drying is an easy way to preserve herbs and chillies

Drying herbs and spices

1

Start Simple

The preserving techniques in this section are easy to master and provide numerous simple ways of capturing the flavours of fresh produce. Choose from a variety of methods, from freezing and bottling to basic jams, pickles, and relishes.

In this section, learn to prepare or make:

Frozen Fruit
pp.20–23

Freezer Jam
pp.24–27

Frozen Veg
pp.28–31

Frozen Herbs
pp.32–33

Pesto
pp.34–41

Vegetables in Oil
pp.42–45

Fruits in Alcohol
pp.46–51

Preserves in Salt *pp.52–55*

Pickles
pp.56–61

Freezer Pickles
pp.62–63

Chutney
pp.64–71

Relish
pp.72–75

How to **Freeze Fresh Fruit**

Freezing is a wonderfully easy way of dramatically slowing down the deterioration of fruit and keeping as much of its flavour and nutrients as possible. It is best to freeze fruit with sugar, as this helps it to retain its texture when thawed. Some fruits can simply be frozen whole, while others need a little basic preparation.

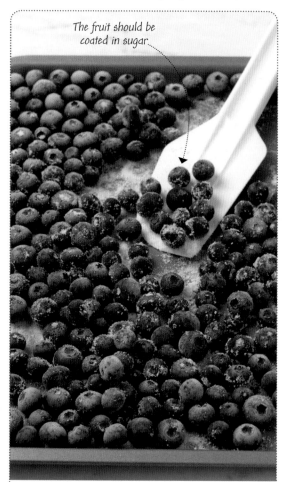

The fruit should be coated in sugar

Open freezing prevents fruit from clumping together

Use small freezer bags

Open-freeze with sugar

Fresh fruits need to be frozen individually first – a procedure called open-freezing – to prevent them from squashing together. Arrange the fruits in a single layer on a baking tray, sprinkle with caster sugar, and put the trays in the freezer.

Pack into freezer bags

It will probably take an hour or so for the fruits to freeze. Once they are completely frozen, remove the trays and pack the fruits into freezer bags, preferably portion-sized freezer bags so you can defrost just a little at a time, as required.

Tip Remove any stones from fruit and cut larger fruit in half or into slices before freezing. Juicy fruit like peaches can be puréed with a little sugar and lemon juice, and frozen in freezer pots. Be sure to leave a small gap at the top of the pot for the purée to expand.

Sugar firms the skins of the fruits as they freeze, helping them retain their shape while frozen and once thawed ....

Only freeze produce that is in good condition

Label and date

Write a "best before" date on each bag. All fruits start spoiling after a certain period in the freezer, so check the table (see p.22) to see how long it can be stored. Freezing breaks down the fruit's cell walls, so it will be squashy when defrosted, but still tasty.

Freezing Times for Fresh Fruit

This table lists the most suitable raw fruits for freezing, the various ways in which you can freeze them, and their maximum storage times. These times are appropriate only if you freeze the fruits below −18°C (0°F). Aim to use them well before these time limits, however, and leave them to thaw in the fridge before using.

Fruits	Freezing Times		
	Sprinkle with sugar and open-freeze on trays (see pp.20–21) *(months)*	Pack in freezer pots, cover in syrup (see p.116) or sugar, and freeze *(months)*	Purée, pack in freezer pots, and freeze *(months)*
Apples	9	9	N/A
Apricots (ripe)	9	9	6
Blackberries	12	12	6
Blackcurrants	12	12	6
Blueberries	12	12	6
Cherries	6	6	6
Citrus fruits	6	N/A	N/A
Cranberries	12	12	6
Figs	9	9	6
Gooseberries	12	12	6
Loganberries	12	12	6
Melons	9	9	6
Nectarines	9	9	6
Peaches	9	9	6
Plums	9	9	6
Raspberries	12	12	6
Rhubarb	12	12	N/A
Strawberries	9	9	6
Fruit syrups (pp.110–11)	Pot up in freezer pots and freeze for 9 months		

Remove the **apricot** stones and cut into halves or slices

Strip the **currants** from their stalks first before open-freezing them

Cut **plums** in half and remove their stones before freezing

Peaches are best frozen in pots as a purée, as the freezing process effectively purées them anyway

Raspberries are an excellent fruit to open-freeze whole

Apples must be peeled, sliced, and dipped in lemon juice first to prevent any discolouration

Open-freezing is the best way to freeze **cranberries** – you can use them straight from the freezer without thawing first

23

How to **Make Freezer Jam**

If you find traditional jams too sweet, or you have very ripe, juicy fruits that would be hard to set as jam, try making freezer jam – a sweetened, uncooked purée thickened with agar, a natural Japanese gelling agent, and frozen to a jelly-like set to preserve its nutrients and flavour. The process is simple and quick, and the results taste refreshing and flavourful.

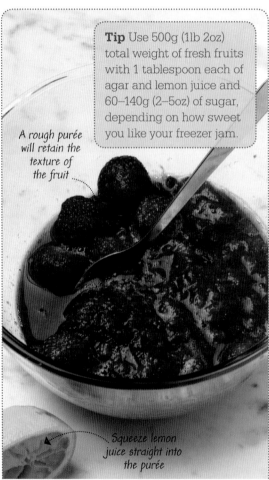

Tip Use 500g (1lb 2oz) total weight of fresh fruits with 1 tablespoon each of agar and lemon juice and 60–140g (2–5oz) of sugar, depending on how sweet you like your freezer jam.

A rough purée will retain the texture of the fruit

Squeeze lemon juice straight into the purée

Agar is made from seaweed, and so is suitable for vegetarians and vegans

Purée the fruit

To prepare the fruit, wash it only if necessary. Put it in a bowl and crush gently with the back of a fork to make a rough, rather than a smooth, purée. You can mix in a tablespoon of lemon juice, which is about half a fresh lemon, for added flavour, if you like.

Dissolve agar and sugar

Sprinkle the agar into a small saucepan of water and leave for 2–3 minutes to soften. Bring slowly to the boil without stirring, and simmer for 3–5 minutes. Stir until the agar dissolves, then add the sugar. Keep stirring for 2–3 minutes until the sugar has dissolved.

Keep stirring the purée as you pour in the agar syrup

Leave a gap of 1cm (½in) at the top of each pot to allow the jam to expand as it freezes

Combine the ingredients

Pour the hot syrup into the bowl of puréed fruit, stirring constantly with a wooden spoon to combine the ingredients thoroughly. It's worth using a spatula to scrape the last of the syrup from the pan into the fruit mixture to ensure the best set.

Pour into freezer pots

The jam thickens rapidly as it cools, so pour it into clean, portion-sized freezer pots before it begins to solidify. Allow the jam to cool in the fridge overnight before sealing and freezing it. To use the jam, thaw, refrigerate, and add to yogurt or desserts, or spread on toast or bread.

Blueberry and Raspberry Freezer Jam

500g   **15 minutes**   **6 months**
(1lb 2oz)

Ingredients

225g (8oz) blueberries

225g (8oz) raspberries

2 tsp lemon juice

1 tbsp agar flakes or 1 tsp agar powder

115g (4oz) caster sugar

CRUSH THE FRUIT

Bring the blueberries and raspberries to room temperature so they release their juices properly and are soft enough to be crushed gently. Then put them in a bowl with the lemon juice and crush roughly with the back of a fork or a potato masher.

Careful! You want to produce a rough purée with plenty of juicy chunks to enjoy.

PREPARE THE AGAR

Sprinkle the agar over 200ml (7fl oz) of water in a small saucepan. Allow the agar to soften for 2–3 minutes before heating the mix gently over a low heat until it comes to the boil. Simmer gently for 3–5 minutes.

Tip Avoid stirring the agar with a spoon while it softens, as this might prevent it from absorbing the water. Instead, agitate the mix by giving the pan a quick swirl just before heating it. Once the mix is boiling, stir it occasionally to make sure the agar has dissolved.

Add the sugar and continue to stir over a low heat for 2–3 minutes until it has completely dissolved: look for any sugar crystals as you stir, just to be sure. Remove the pan from the heat.

MIX THE SYRUP AND THE FRUIT

Pour the agar syrup into the bowl of crushed berries. Stir constantly but gently to combine.

POT UP THE JAM

Pour the jam into clean, portion-sized freezer pots. Allow at least 1cm (½in) of space at the top. Allow to cool, then seal, label, and refrigerate overnight before freezing. To use, thaw in the fridge overnight first, then keep refrigerated and consume within 2 weeks.

Strawberry Freezer Jam

**600g
(1lb 5oz)**   **15 minutes**   **6 months**

Ingredients

500g (1lb 2oz) strawberries, washed only
    if necessary

1 tsp lemon juice

1 tbsp agar flakes or 1 tsp agar powder

60–115g (2–4oz) caster sugar

CRUSH THE FRUIT

Roughly crush the strawberries in a bowl
with the lemon juice using the back of a fork or
a potato masher.

Careful! Avoid crushing the fruit too fiercely.

PREPARE THE AGAR

Sprinkle the agar over 200ml (7fl oz) of water in
a small saucepan. Allow the agar to soften for 2–3
minutes before heating gently over a low heat until
it comes to the boil. Simmer gently for 3–5 minutes.

Tip Stirring the agar as it softens may prevent
it from absorbing the water. Instead, just give the
pan a quick swirl before heating, to agitate the
mix. Once the mix is boiling, stir it occasionally
until the agar dissolves.

Add the sugar and continue to stir over a low
heat for 2–3 minutes until it has all dissolved and
you can't see any more sugar crystals in the
solution. Remove the pan from the heat.

MIX THE SYRUP AND THE FRUIT

Pour the agar syrup into the bowl of crushed
strawberries. Stir constantly but gently to combine.

POT UP THE JAM

Pour the jam into clean, portion-sized freezer
pots. Allow at least 1cm (½in) of space at the top.
Allow to cool, then seal, label, refrigerate overnight
to thicken fully, and freeze. To use, thaw in the
fridge overnight first, then keep refrigerated and
consume within 2 weeks.

How to **Freeze Blanched Vegetables**

Freezing is one of the most convenient ways to preserve vegetables, and the results are worth it: thawed frozen produce tastes almost as fresh as it does when picked. Some vegetables need to be blanched (briefly cooked in water) before freezing to destroy the enzymes that can cause their colour, flavour, and texture to deteriorate.

Keep the water at a rolling boil as you add the vegetables

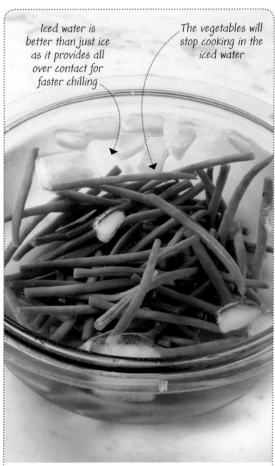

Iced water is better than just ice as it provides all over contact for faster chilling

The vegetables will stop cooking in the iced water

Blanch the vegetables

Boil a pan of lightly salted water and add a small handful of vegetables. Bring quickly back to the boil, and cook the vegetables for 2–3 minutes. Cook the vegetables in small batches, so the water boils soon after the vegetables have been added. Repeat until all vegetables are done.

Ice and drain

Transfer each batch of vegetables immediately to a bowl of iced water to halt the cooking process. Then drain the vegetables and pat them dry with kitchen paper. Dry the vegetables thoroughly before freezing; the firmer and less watery their texture, the better they will freeze.

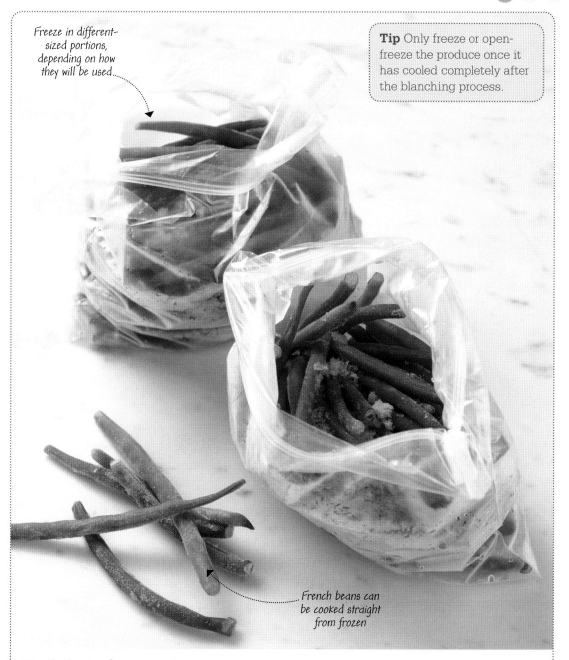

Freeze in different-
sized portions,
depending on how
they will be used...

Tip Only freeze or open-
freeze the produce once it
has cooled completely after
the blanching process.

French beans can
be cooked straight
from frozen

Pack into freezer bags

When the vegetables are dry, pack them
in convenient portions in freezer bags or
containers. If you want to freeze larger

batches, open-freeze them first (see p.20) to
prevent them sticking together and then
store them in large freezer bags.

Freezing Times for Blanched Vegetables

This table lists the most suitable vegetables for freezing, how to prepare them, how long to blanch them for, and their maximum storage times. However, you should aim to use the produce well before these time limits. Ensure that you freeze all produce below –18°C (0°F). All these vegetables, apart from sweetcorn cobs, can be cooked straight from the freezer.

Vegetables	How to prepare	Blanch (minutes)	Freeze (months)
Asparagus	Trim	2–4	9
Beans, broad	Pod	2–3	12
Beans, French	Leave whole	2–3	9
Beans, runner (tender)	Slice	2	9
Broccoli florets	Separate	2	9
Brussels sprouts	Leave whole	3	9
Cabbages	Slice	2	6
Carrots (small)	Leave whole	5	9
Carrots	Slice	2–3	9
Cauliflower florets	Separate	3	6
Fennel	Slice	2	6
Globe artichokes (bottoms)	Leave whole	4	9
Globe artichokes (baby)	Leave whole	3	9
Mangetout	Leave whole	1	9
Peas	Pod	1–2	12
Romanesco florets	Separate	2	9
Salsify/scorzonera	Peel, chop	2–3	9
Sugarsnap peas	Leave whole	2	9
Spinach	Wash	1	9
Sweetcorn (cobs)	Leave whole	6	12
Sweetcorn (kernels)	Separate	2	12
Swiss chard (leaves/stalks)	Wash, chop	1–2	9

Top and tail, slice, blanch, and open-freeze **runner beans** before storing them in the freezer

Scrubbed **carrots** are best sliced in matchsticks or rounds before being blanched and frozen

Cut **romanesco and cauliflowers** into small florets before blanching and freezing

Broad beans store very well after open-freezing, retaining all their texture

Blanch **spinach** briefly and then squeeze gently to remove the moisture before packing into freezer bags

Blanch and freeze whole **sweetcorn** cobs, or stand the cobs upright, run a sharp knife down the sides to strip off the kernels, and blanch the kernels before freezing

How to **Freeze Herbs**

Preserving delicate herbs by freezing them guarantees you can always include their fresh, fragrant flavours, essential oils, and colours in dishes. However, the freezing process does affect their texture, so they are best frozen in oil or water for ease of use. Add them in the same quantities as fresh herbs – they are not concentrated in flavour like dried herbs.

Preserve in oil

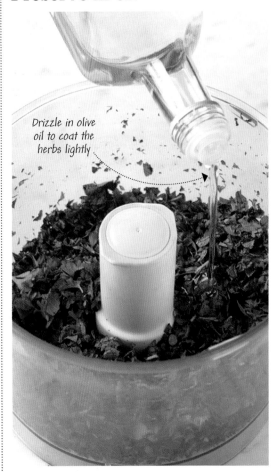

Drizzle in olive oil to coat the herbs lightly

CHOP AND ADD OIL
Fresh herb leaves become limp when frozen, so strip them from their stalks, put in a food processor, and blitz until finely chopped. Add 1 tablespoon of extra virgin olive oil for every 3 tablespoons of chopped herbs.

PACK INTO FREEZER BAGS
Divide the chopped herb mixture into batches and spoon each batch into very small freezer bags. Herbs in oil freeze well for up to 4 months. Good herbs to preserve in oil include basil, parsley, and coriander.

Preserve in water

Chop the leaves so they are easier to handle when defrosted

CHOP FINELY

Ice-cube trays provide an excellent way to freeze herbs such as chives, parsley, tarragon, dill, chervil, and coriander. Strip the leaves from their stalks and blitz briefly in a food processor. Alternatively, you could finely chop the herbs by hand.

Tip Frozen herbs work well in salad dressings, hot dishes, sauces, stuffings, and toppings. If you make frozen ice cubes, you can pop them straight from the freezer into pans of hot food. Use the ice cubes within 6 months.

Each ice cube contains about 1 tablespoon of chopped herbs

FILL THE TRAY

Fill each ice-cube hole up to the brim with chopped herbs and pour on just enough water to cover. Put the tray in the freezer for about 2 hours, or until the herb cubes have frozen. Then knock them out of the tray and divide up into small freezer bags.

How to **Make Pesto**

Pesto is an intensely flavoured paste of ground aromatic herbs, or strong spices, combined with oil and a strong cheese such as Parmesan. Pesto is not a long-lasting preserve because it contains no significant levels of salt, vinegar, or sugar, but sealing it with a layer of oil to exclude the air will allow you to store it for up to 2 weeks.

Tip Add just enough olive oil to give you the desired consistency. Don't be afraid to add a little extra oil, if you like a more fluid pesto, or less, if you want it firmer.

Pour in just enough oil to make a glistening paste

Using a food processor

The quickest and least laborious way to make pesto is in a food processor. You can quickly blitz all the dry ingredients and add the oil while the processor is still running, to create a smooth, fine-textured paste. However, take care not to add too much oil at once.

Press the pestle down firmly and stir it around the mortar

Pound the basil, toasted pine nuts, and garlic first, before adding the cheese

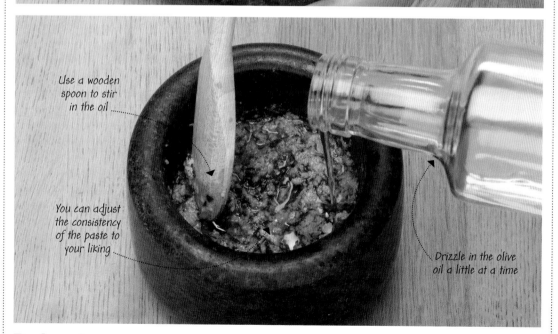

Use a wooden spoon to stir in the oil

You can adjust the consistency of the paste to your liking

Drizzle in the olive oil a little at a time

By hand

Pesto can also be made in a pestle and mortar, although it requires a lot of elbow grease! It gives the pesto a more robust texture and allows you more time to judge the amount of oil needed to bind the mixture to your desired consistency. Season to taste and serve.

Basil Pesto

A traditional pesto that derives from Genoa, Italy, this
pungently flavoured condiment made with fresh basil
leaves is extremely easy to make, and very quick if you
own a food processor. It tastes divine simply tossed
with pasta or added to crushed new potatoes.

1 small jar | **Approx. 10–15 minutes** | **2 weeks (2 months, if frozen)**

Ingredients

25g (scant 1oz) pine nuts

60g (2oz) basil leaves

1 large clove garlic, peeled

40g (1½oz) Parmesan cheese, finely grated

90ml (3fl oz) extra virgin olive oil, plus extra for sealing the pesto

sea salt

freshly ground black pepper

Equipment

frying pan

wooden spoon

food processor or pestle and mortar

airtight jar with lid

pine nuts

basil leaves

garlic clove

Parmesan cheese

extra virgin olive oil

sea salt

black pepper

frying pan

wooden spoon

food processor

airtight jar with lid

37

1 Dry fry the pine nuts in a clean frying pan and cook over a low heat for 2–3 minutes, stirring frequently until just toasted but not coloured. Remove from the heat.

Careful! Nuts can burn very quickly. Keep the heat low, keep stirring, and don't leave them unattended. Dry-frying pine nuts helps to release their flavour, but if allowed to colour they will lose their creaminess when processed.

Wash and gently dry the basil leaves, if needed, before chopping them

2 Place the pine nuts, basil, and garlic in a food processor and blitz until almost smooth. Alternatively, use a pestle and mortar (see p.35).

Tip Use a spatula intermittently to scrape down the sides of the processor so all the ingredients are evenly processed.

3 Add the Parmesan cheese to the processor. Keep it running and slowly add the extra virgin olive oil through the feed tube until it is all incorporated.

Help! Don't worry about over-working the ingredients while you keep the processor running. The flavour of the pesto won't suffer from being finely blended.

Drizzle the olive oil gradually into the processor so it combines well with the other ingredients

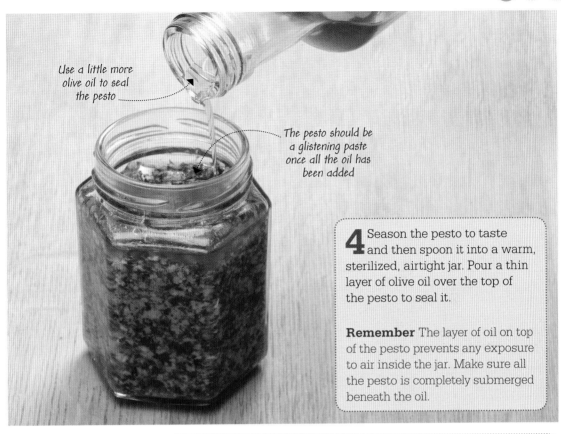

Use a little more olive oil to seal the pesto

The pesto should be a glistening paste once all the oil has been added

4 Season the pesto to taste and then spoon it into a warm, sterilized, airtight jar. Pour a thin layer of olive oil over the top of the pesto to seal it.

Remember The layer of oil on top of the pesto prevents any exposure to air inside the jar. Make sure all the pesto is completely submerged beneath the oil.

How to store

You can store the pesto in the fridge for up to 2 weeks.

If you make a lot of pesto, you can freeze it in small freezer pots or ice-cube trays for up to 2 months. Just remember to leave out the Parmesan cheese from the ingredients, because it loses its flavour when frozen. Before serving, defrost the pesto and stir in the required quantity of grated Parmesan cheese.

Did anything go wrong?

The basil in the pesto discoloured. It has been exposed to the air too long and oxidized.

Next time, take care to store the fresh pesto in an airtight container and cover completely with oil. This prevents the pesto from getting oxidized.

Use only very fresh herbs, making sure you discard any stems or leaves that are tinged brown.

Other combinations

The Italian word "pesto" roughly translates as "pounded" and does not refer to any one recipe. There are plenty of variations of pesto you could try. Parsley and walnuts go well together, as do rocket, basil, parsley, and chives with cashew nuts, while wild garlic leaves and pine nuts make a fabulous seasonal combination.

Try more Pesto recipes ▶ ▶ ▶

Coriander and Walnut Pesto

1 small jar   **10 minutes**   **2 weeks, refrigerated**

Ingredients

approx. 30g (1oz) bunch of fresh coriander

1 large garlic clove, peeled

30g (1oz) walnut pieces

a good grinding of black pepper

a good pinch of salt

30g (1oz) Parmesan cheese, freshly grated

5 tbsp extra virgin olive oil

PROCESS THE INGREDIENTS

Trim the stalks from the coriander and lightly crush the garlic clove by pressing it under the side of the blade of a large chopping knife. Put the coriander leaves in a food processor with the other ingredients and 1 tablespoon of the oil and blitz for a few seconds.

Remember If you prefer a rougher paste, you can make the pesto in a pestle and mortar (see p.35).

ADD THE OIL

Gradually add the remaining oil while keeping the food processor running until the ingredients form a glistening paste.

POT UP IN A JAR

Spoon the pesto into a sterilized jar, making sure you don't leave any air pockets, and pour a little oil over the surface to exclude any air. Seal, label, and store in the fridge.

Remember It's important to cover the pesto surface completely with oil to keep out airborne microbes and to starve any microbes in the pesto of air. If you don't use up all the pesto for one meal, cover what is left in the jar with about a tablespoon or so of olive oil and screw the lid back on tightly.

Rocket Pesto

1 small jar **15 minutes** **2 weeks, refrigerated**

Ingredients

30g (1oz) rocket, washed

1 garlic clove, peeled

30g (1oz) blue cheese, crumbled or diced, depending on the texture

45g (1½oz) blanched, toasted almonds

4 tbsp extra virgin olive oil

salt and freshly ground black pepper

PROCESS THE INGREDIENTS

Put the rocket in a food processor and lightly crush the garlic clove by pressing it under the side of a large chopping knife. Add the garlic, cheese, almonds, and 2 tablespoons of the oil to the food processor and blitz for a few seconds.

Remember You can make the pesto in a pestle and mortar for a rougher texture (see p.35).

ADD THE OIL

Gradually add the remaining oil while keeping the food processor running until the ingredients form a glistening paste. Season to taste with salt and freshly ground pepper.

POT UP IN A JAR

Spoon the pesto into a sterilized jar, making sure you don't leave any air pockets, and pour a little oil over the surface to exclude any air. Seal, label, and store in the fridge.

Remember It's important to cover the surface of the pesto completely with oil to keep out airborne microbes and to starve any microbes in the pesto of air. If you don't use up all the pesto for one meal, cover what is left over with about a tablespoon or so of olive oil and screw the lid back on tightly.

How to **Prepare Vegetables in Oil**

Oil is not a preservative but an air excluder, or sealant, protecting the produce against airborne microbes and starving aerobic bacteria. It also brings out the flavour of many vegetables, so it is worth storing fresh produce in oil for short periods of time. However, it is important to process the vegetables first, to kill any microorganisms that may otherwise survive.

Acidify the vegetables

Boil the chopped vegetables with sugar, salt, and just enough vinegar to cover them until soft on the outside but very firm in the centre. The acid in vinegar prevents the growth of most microbes. Heating destroys microbes and the enzymes that trigger deterioration.

Pour in the oil

Pour enough olive oil into the jars to cover the vegetables, to prevent the air coming into contact with the food. The oil starves aerobic bacteria of the oxygen they need to survive. Press the vegetables down gently to expel any trapped air pockets.

Italian-style Vegetables

2 medium jars | **30 minutes, plus 1 week** | **1–2 months, refrigerated**

Ingredients

600g (1lb 5oz) mixed seasonal vegetables

about 500ml (16fl oz) white wine vinegar

2 tsp granulated sugar

2 tsp sea salt

approx. 150ml (5fl oz) extra virgin olive oil

seasonings (dried fennel seeds, dried oregano, bay leaf, rosemary, lemon thyme, chilli flakes)

CHOP THE VEGETABLES

Wash and peel the vegetables, if necessary, and slice each into evenly sized pieces about 1cm (½in) thick.

Tip Chop vegetables such as aubergines, fennel, small florets of cauliflower or romanesco, courgettes, celery, carrots, French beans, and peppers. Leave small shallots and mushrooms whole.

BLANCH IN VINEGAR

Put a small batch of the sliced vegetables in a stainless-steel saucepan and pour in just enough vinegar to cover. Add the sugar and salt and bring to the boil.

Boil the vegetable slices in batches until *al dente* (soft on the outside but firm in the centre): about 2–3 minutes for tender vegetables and 5–10 minutes for firmer ones. To test, cool a piece of vegetable under water before trying it with your teeth, pinching it between two fingers, or cutting it in half with a knife. Then lift the vegetables from the pan with a slotted spoon, pat dry with kitchen paper, and allow to cool. Repeat this process with the remaining vegetables.

PACK INTO JARS

Pack the vegetables into sterilized jars and add some seasonings. Choose from 1 teaspoon dried fennel seeds, 1 teaspoon dried oregano, 1 fresh or dried bay leaf, 1 sprig rosemary, 1 sprig lemon thyme, or a pinch of chilli flakes. Cover with olive oil and tap the jars lightly on a work surface to remove any air bubbles. Top up with more oil to cover completely. Seal and label the jars, and store in the fridge. Leave for at least 1 week before opening to allow the flavours to develop. Top up with more oil as needed so the vegetables are always covered.

Careful! Make sure the surfaces of the vegetables are not exposed to the air to keep out airborne microbes.

Mixed Peppers in Oil

2 medium jars   **40 minutes**   **3–4 weeks, refrigerated**

Ingredients

3 red peppers

3 orange peppers

3 yellow peppers

1 tsp dried oregano

sea salt

freshly ground black pepper

2 tbsp extra virgin olive oil, plus extra to top up

2 tbsp cider vinegar

ROAST THE PEPPERS

Preheat the oven to 200°C (400°F/Gas 6). Arrange the peppers in a roasting tray and roast in the oven for 20–30 minutes until they are lightly charred – the skin will pucker up from the flesh and start to burn in patches. Immediately, while the peppers are still hot, place them inside sandwich or freezer bags. Tie the bags closed and allow the peppers to cool.

Why? The steam trapped inside the bags will help loosen the skins and make the peppers easier to peel.

PREPARE THE PEPPERS

Cut the peppers in half and scrape out the seeds. Now remove the skin and any stalks.

Slice the flesh roughly into strips, then place in a bowl, and add the oregano, salt, and black pepper. Mix the oil and vinegar together, pour it into the bowl, and combine with the peppers.

POT UP IN JARS

Spoon the peppers into sterilized jars and pour in the juices from the bowl. Add enough olive oil to cover the peppers completely. Seal and label the jars, and refrigerate. Top up with more oil as needed, making sure the vegetables are always covered. Use within 1 month.

Artichokes in Oil

1 small jar   45 minutes   2 months, refrigerated

Ingredients

10 baby artichokes

300ml (10fl oz) white wine vinegar

1 tbsp sea salt

thyme sprigs (optional)

For the marinade

450ml (15fl oz) extra virgin olive oil

75ml (2½fl oz) white wine vinegar

handful of black peppercorns

PREPARE THE ARTICHOKES

Trim the stalks of the artichokes and remove the outer leaves (about 5–6 layers), leaving the paler, more tender leaves. Trim off about 2.5cm (1in) from the tops and discard. The fuzzy, silky mass of immature florets at the centre of the artichoke is known as the "choke" and is unpleasant to eat. Remove the choke to expose the succulent heart beneath. Leave whole or cut in half.

BLANCH THE ARTICHOKES

Put the vinegar and salt in a preserving pan or heavy-based stainless-steel saucepan. Add 300ml (10fl oz) of water and bring to the boil. Add the artichokes and simmer for 3–5 minutes until *al dente*. Drain, leave to cool, and cut lengthways into quarters.

Remember The acid in the vinegar prevents the growth of most microbes. Heating also destroys microbes and the enzymes that trigger deterioration.

PREPARE THE MARINADE

Place the marinade ingredients in a pan and bring to the boil. Add the artichokes to the mix. Bring back to the boil, then turn off the heat. Allow the artichokes to cool in the marinade.

PACK INTO JARS

Put the artichokes into a sterilized jar with a non-metallic or vinegar-proof lid. Add the thyme sprigs, if you are using them. Pour in all the marinade to cover the vegetables completely. Seal and label the jars, and refrigerate.

Careful! As you consume the artichokes keep topping up the jar with oil as needed to ensure the artichokes are not exposed to the air. Use within 2 months.

How to **Bottle Fruits in Alcohol**

Fresh fruits bottled in alcohol are possibly the easiest preserves to prepare and will keep almost indefinitely, as no microorganisms can grow in high concentrations of alcohol. The combination of succulent, sweet fruit and alcohol, such as brandy, rum, whisky, vodka, or gin, makes for one of the most delicious and indulgent of treats.

Bottling in cold alcohol

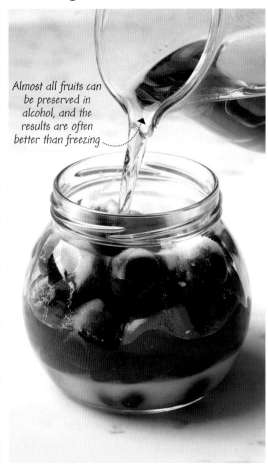

Almost all fruits can be preserved in alcohol, and the results are often better than freezing

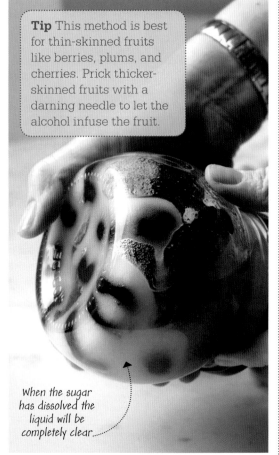

Tip This method is best for thin-skinned fruits like berries, plums, and cherries. Prick thicker-skinned fruits with a darning needle to let the alcohol infuse the fruit.

When the sugar has dissolved the liquid will be completely clear

ADD SUGAR AND ALCOHOL
Gently pack the fresh fruit into a wide-necked sterilized preserving jar without bruising or squashing them. Add enough sugar to fill one-third of the jar and then pour in enough alcohol to completely cover the fruit.

DISSOLVE THE SUGAR
Tap the jar lightly on the work surface to expel any air bubbles, and then seal the jar. The sugar will gradually dissolve in the alcohol, but give the jar an occasional shake to help it dissolve completely.

Combining with hot syrup

You can adjust the sugar content in the syrup to taste, depending on how tart the fruit is

MAKE A SUGAR SYRUP

Put cold water in a large saucepan, add sugar (115–250g/4–10oz per 600ml/1 pint total liquid), and heat gently, stirring continuously until all the sugar crystals have dissolved. Bring to the boil and simmer for 5 minutes. Submerge the fruit in the syrup and return to the boil.

Tie the spice bag with a long piece of string so it's easier to remove

POACH THE FRUIT AND FLAVOUR THE SYRUP

Reduce the heat and briefly poach the fruit according to the recipe. Lift out the fruit with a slotted spoon and leave to cool. If you like, you can flavour the syrup after poaching by adding a muslin spice bag of whole spices (see p.57). Bring the syrup back to the boil and boil rapidly for a few minutes. Allow to cool slightly before adding to the jar and topping up with alcohol.

Apricots and Almonds in Amaretto

1 large jar   20 minutes, plus 4 weeks   12 months

Ingredients

85g (3oz) granulated sugar

450g (1lb) apricots, halved and stoned

60g (2oz) blanched almonds

approx. 250ml (8fl oz) amaretto

Tip If you prefer to skin the apricots before bottling them, plunge the whole fruits into a bowl of boiling water for 1 minute, then a bowl of cold water, and peel off the skins (see p.28).

MAKE THE SYRUP

Heat the sugar and 150ml (5fl oz) water in a large saucepan over a low heat, stirring until the sugar has all dissolved.

Careful! Make sure you can't see any more sugar crystals in the solution.

BLANCH THE APRICOTS

Put half the apricots in the pan to form a single layer in the syrup. Bring to the boil, and boil for 1 minute until the apricots are slightly soft but still hold their shape.

Remember Boiling the apricots in batches like this means that the water comes back to the boil quickly, and the fruits are covered and cook evenly.

Transfer the apricots to a sterilized jar with a slotted spoon and add half the almonds. Repeat with the rest of the batch.

ADD THE SYRUP AND AMARETTO

Put the pan back on the heat, bring the syrup to the boil, and pour it into the jar. Add enough amaretto to cover the apricots completely. Leave to cool. Seal and label the jar, then gently tip it upside down a couple of times to combine the syrup and alcohol. Store in a cool, dark place for 4 weeks for the flavours to mature, and refrigerate after opening.

Cherries in Brandy

3 small jars | **10 minutes, plus 4 weeks** | **12 months or longer**

Ingredients

500g (1lb 2oz) just-ripe sweet or Morello cherries, washed and de-stalked

approx. 175g (6oz) caster sugar

approx. 350ml (12fl oz) brandy

FILL THE JARS WITH FRUIT

Discard any fruits that are not in perfect condition, then pack the rest into wide-necked sterilized preserving jars.

Help! If you are worried about how much fruit to pack into each jar, aim to add as many as you can without squashing or bruising them.

ADD SUGAR AND ALCOHOL

Add enough sugar to fill one-third of each jar. Pour in enough brandy to fill the jar completely and cover the fruit.

Tip Try to keep a ratio of ¼–⅓ sugar to ¾–⅔ alcohol when filling the jars to ensure that all the sugar dissolves in the alcohol and you don't end up with a gritty liqueur.

EXPEL AIR BUBBLES

Tap each jar gently on a work surface to release any air pockets and to ensure that no airborne microorganisms within the trapped air bubbles come into contact with the food and spoil it. Then seal, label, and store the jars in a cool, dark place.

DISSOLVE THE SUGAR AND MATURE

Occasionally turn the jars upside down over the next few days, or give them a shake to help the sugar dissolve in the alcohol. Store in a cool, dark place for 4 weeks to allow the flavours to mature, and refrigerate after opening.

Plums in Brandy variation Use the same quantities of plums, caster sugar, and brandy. Prick the plums with a fork or darning needle before bowand if the plums are quite large, halve and stone them instead.

Kumquats in Vodka

1 large jar   10 minutes, plus 2–3 months   12 months

Ingredients

500g (1lb 2oz) kumquats, washed, scrubbed, and dried

6 cardamom pods (optional)

approx. 175g (6oz) caster sugar

approx. 360ml (12fl oz) vodka

Special Equipment

cocktail stick or darning needle

FILL THE JARS WITH FRUIT

Prick the kumquats all over with a cocktail stick or darning needle, and pack into a sterilized preserving jar without squashing or bruising them.

Why? Pricking the fruit is vital as it allows the vodka syrup to penetrate the fruit, both preserving it and saturating it with flavour.

If you are using cardamom pods, crush them lightly with a pestle or the side of a knife. You want to split them without releasing the seeds.

ADD SUGAR AND ALCOHOL

Add enough sugar to fill one-third of the jar, then top up the jar with vodka so it completely covers the fruit.

Tip Try to keep a ratio of ¼–⅓ sugar to ¾–⅔ alcohol when filling the jar of fruit.

EXPEL AIR BUBBLES

Tap the jar gently on a work surface to release any air pockets, then seal and label. For the next few days, occasionally turn the jar upside down or give it a shake to help the sugar dissolve in the alcohol. Store in a cool, dark place for 2–3 months for the flavours to mature. Once opened, refrigerate and eat within 2 weeks.

Sloe Gin

1 large bottle | **20 minutes, plus 3 months** | **12 months**

Ingredients

approx. 225g (8oz) sloes, fresh or frozen (thawed to room temperature, if frozen)

85g (3oz) caster sugar

4 juniper berries, slightly crushed

a few drops of natural almond extract

approx. 350ml (12fl oz) gin

Special Equipment

cocktail stick or darning needle

FILL THE JARS WITH FRUIT

Prick each sloe with a cocktail stick or darning needle. If you are using frozen sloes, there is no need to prick them.

Why? Pricking the sloes releases more of their flavour. If you find this process too fiddly, simply freeze the sloes beforehand for a few hours instead – the freezing process softens the skins. If you are picking sloes after the first frosts, you similarly may not need to prick them.

Put the sloes in a sterilized bottle.

ADD SUGAR AND ALCOHOL

Add the sugar, juniper berries, and almond extract. Pour in enough gin to fill the bottle and cover the fruit. Seal and label the bottle.

Tip This recipe uses less sugar than some, so increase the quantities of sugar if you prefer a sweeter liqueur.

MIX THE INGREDIENTS

Shake the bottle gently or tip it upside down a few times to combine all the ingredients. Leave in a cool, dark place for 3 months, shaking the bottle occasionally.

STRAIN THE LIQUEUR

Strain the sloe gin into a sterilized bottle, seal, and use as required.

Damson Gin variation If you prefer (or if sloes aren't available), you can substitute damsons for sloes. Keep all the quantities and all the other ingredients the same, but remember you may need a wider-necked bottle.

How to **Make Simple Salt Preserves**

Lemons and certain vegetables make delicious salted preserves; they develop a mellow, tangy flavour and softer texture. Most salted vegetables will last for several weeks or months if they are stored in the fridge; lemons should last for 6–9 months.

Use coarse sea salt to make the brine

Scrub waxed lemons with a vegetable brush to remove any wax

Salting in a colander

Some vegetables, such as cabbage, are preserved simply by drawing out their moisture with salt. Put the sliced vegetables in a large colander. Sprinkle salt over them and use your hands to toss the ingredients together; work in the salt thoroughly until the vegetable slices start to feel wet. Set the colander over a bowl and leave to stand at room temperature overnight. The bowl will catch the juice dripping from the vegetable.

Making a slow, cold brine

Tightly pack the fruit or vegetables into the jar. Add a generous amount of salt over each layer and into any gaps until you have used the amount recommended by the recipe. Fill the jar to the brim with boiled, cooled water, then seal it. Then, to encourage the salt to begin dissolving, gently shake the jar. Repeat this process every day for 2 weeks. The salt will gradually dissolve into the water to form brine.

Pour in enough brine to fill the jar to the brim and cover the vegetables completely

Make sure the brine is boiling as you pour it into the jar, to keep it sterile

Careful! Avoid using jars with unlined metal lids when potting up: the lids will corrode and spoil the preserve. Always use jars with vinegar-proof lids, which have plasticized linings. For the best possible results, choose new lids, even if you recycle the jars.

Making a hot brine

This technique ensures the salt is dissolved from the start, by putting it in a saucepan with the water and heating gently, stirring until all the salt dissolves. Bring the brine to the boil and pour over a sterilized jar packed with the vegetables and any flavourings.

Preserved Lemons

1 large jar | **10 minutes, plus 3–4 weeks** | **6–9 months, in the fridge**

Ingredients

4 unwaxed lemons

115g (4oz) coarse sea salt

a few bay leaves

½ tsp black peppercorns

1 dried chilli

a few cloves, or coriander or cumin
seeds (optional)

freshly squeezed juice of 2 extra lemons

CUT THE LEMONS

Make a deep cut through each lemon from
the top, stopping two-thirds of the way down.
Then make a second deep cut at a right angle
to the first, so you end up with 4 lemon quarters
joined at the base.

PACK WITH SALT

Open out the cut quarters slightly and pack
salt into each crevice. Place the filled lemons in
a sterilized preserving jar and add the seasonings.
Add the remaining salt to the jar.

MAKE THE BRINE

Pour in the lemon juice and top up with
cooled, boiled water, if needed, to cover the lemons
and fill the jar completely. Seal and store at room
temperature. Leave for 3–4 weeks for the lemon
rinds to soften. Shake or tip the jar upside down
occasionally to help the salt to dissolve and form
a brine. You can use the salted lemons in salads,
sauces, vinaigrettes, salsas or tagines.

Salted Cucumbers with Dill

1 large jar | 30 minutes, plus 4–6 weeks | 2 weeks, refrigerated once opened

Ingredients

30g (1oz) sea salt

4 tbsp dill, chopped

1 tbsp tarragon, chopped

1 tsp black peppercorns

1 tsp celery seeds

2 ridge cucumbers, about 18cm (7in) long, quartered lengthways, or approx. 8 small whole pickling cucumbers

4 pickling onions or shallots, peeled and thickly sliced

MAKE THE BRINE

Put the salt and 600ml (1 pint) water into a saucepan and heat gently, stirring until the salt has dissolved and you can see no more salt crystals in the water. Bring to the boil and remove from the heat.

FILL THE JARS

Place half the fresh herbs, peppercorns, and celery seeds in the base of a sterilized preserving jar. Pack the cucumber quarters and sliced onions on top, and cover with the remaining herbs.

POUR IN THE BRINE

Add enough boiling brine to cover the cucumbers and flavourings completely. Seal, label, and store in a cool, dark place for 4–6 weeks. Once opened, store in the fridge.

Kimchi

450–600g (1lb–1lb 5oz) | 25 minutes, plus 4–5 days | 2 weeks, refrigerated

Ingredients

1 small head Chinese leaves, cut into 5cm (2in) chunks

2 tbsp sea salt

4 spring onions, chopped

2.5cm (1in) piece of fresh root ginger, peeled and grated

1 garlic clove, crushed

4 tbsp rice vinegar

1 tbsp Thai fish sauce (*nam pla*)

juice of 1 lime

2 tbsp sesame oil

2 tbsp toasted sesame seeds

2 tbsp sambal oelek

Special Equipment

large plastic container

SALT THE LEAVES

Put the chopped leaves into a colander set over a bowl. Add the salt and mix thoroughly with your hands until the cabbage is well coated.

Leave to stand overnight at room temperature. Next day, wash the leaves in water to remove all the salt. Drain and dry thoroughly on kitchen paper. Transfer to the plastic container, add the rest of the ingredients, and combine well. Seal.

MARINATE THE LEAVES

Leave overnight to marinate at room temperature, then chill in the fridge for another few days. Keep refrigerated and use within 2 weeks.

How to **Make Pickles**

Pickling means to store produce in vinegar, which is a very effective preservative. A simple pickling process transforms fruit and vegetables into crisp, crunchy, versatile condiments with piquancy and bite. It's an easy two-stage process: salting or brining to draw out moisture, then submerging the produce in hot or cold vinegar.

Salting

To keep the pickled produce crisp, you need to remove its excess water. Put a layer of salt in a bowl and top with a layer of vegetable slices. Repeat the process, finishing with a good sprinkling of salt. Leave the bowl at room temperature for 24 hours, then wash off all the salt.

Dry salting is ideal for watery vegetables such as cucumbers, as it helps firm them up

Brining

Soaking in brine is best for less juicy produce. Dissolve salt in cold water to make a saline solution. Put the vegetables in a bowl and pour in enough solution to cover them completely. Leave in a cool place to soak for 12–48 hours. Then rinse the vegetables. Removing some moisture from the vegetables also prevents the vinegar from becoming diluted, which would make it a less effective preservative.

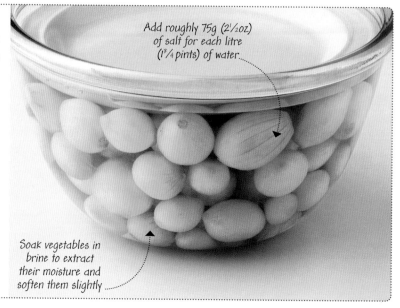

Add roughly 75g (2½oz) of salt for each litre (1¾ pints) of water

Soak vegetables in brine to extract their moisture and soften them slightly

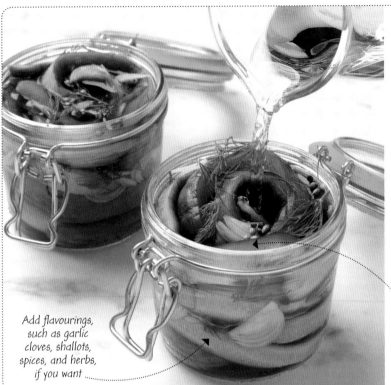

Cold Pickling

Pack the vegetables into wide-necked sterilized jars. To make a crisp cold pickle, simply pour in enough cold vinegar to cover the vegetables completely, leaving a gap of 1cm (½in) at the top of the jar. Seal the jars with non-metallic or vinegar-proof lids.

Pack the vegetables into the jars without overfilling them or pressing them down too tightly

Add flavourings, such as garlic cloves, shallots, spices, and herbs, if you want

Place dried herbs on a square of muslin and tie with string

Make string long enough so it's easy to remove

Hot pickling

Use hot vinegar to give the pickled produce a softer texture, and add a spice bag for flavour. Boil the vinegar in a saucepan for about 5 minutes until it reduces by about a third, then carefully pour into the jars right up to the brim, so the vegetables are completely covered. Seal with non-metallic or vinegar-proof lids.

Pickled Gherkins

| 2 small jars | 1 day, plus 3–4 weeks | 6 months or longer |

Ingredients

500g (1lb 2oz) small pickling cucumbers, washed well and rubbed with a cloth to dry and remove their fine down

125g (4½oz) sea salt

3–4 shallots, peeled

3–4 garlic cloves, peeled (optional)

2–3 dried chillies (optional)

½ tsp each coriander seeds, peppercorns, and dill seeds, or 1 crumbled dried bay leaf

2 sprigs dill, tarragon, or thyme

1 washed vine leaf (optional)

approx. 750ml (1¼ pints) white wine vinegar

PREPARE THE CUCUMBERS

Cut off any stalks and dried blossoms. Quarter the cucumbers lengthways, or cut into 3mm (⅛in) slices, if they can't fit whole into the jars.

SALT THE CUCUMBERS

Put a little of the salt in a glass or ceramic bowl and add a layer of cucumbers. Cover the layer with more salt, and repeat the process until all the cucumbers are arranged in the bowl. Sprinkle the last of the sea salt over the top. Leave for 24 hours at room temperature.

Remember By salting the cucumbers you are extracting some of their liquid and firming them up. This prevents excess water from being released into the jar and diluting the vinegar.

PACK INTO JARS

Wash the cucumbers to rinse off the salt and pack into sterilized jars, leaving 1cm (½in) head space. Add the shallots, garlic cloves (if using), spices, and herbs. Use dill for a classic flavour and a vine leaf for crunch – the tannins in the leaves help keep the pickles crisp.

ADD THE VINEGAR

Pour in enough vinegar to cover the cucumbers completely. Seal with non-metallic or vinegar-proof lids, label, and store in a cool, dark place for 3–4 weeks, to mature.

Tip Remove the pickles with wooden tongs rather than a fork or spoon to prevent them from developing a metallic taste.

Mixed Vegetable Pickle

2 medium jars | **1 day, plus 10 days** | **3 months, refrigerated**

Ingredients

1 litre (1¾ pints) white wine vinegar

mixed whole spices (see method)

60g (2oz) sea salt

1 small cauliflower, chopped into florets

1 large onion, roughly chopped

2 carrots, peeled and sliced

10 cherry tomatoes

5 jalapeño peppers, left whole (optional)

1 tsp coriander seeds

1 tsp mustard seeds

MAKE THE PICKLING VINEGAR

Place a selection of spices in a square of muslin. You can use whatever whole spices you have to hand or all or any of the following: 1 tablespoon black peppercorns, ½ teaspoon cloves, 1 teaspoon crumbed mace blades, 1 tablespoon allspice berries, 1 tablespoon mustard seeds, 1 crushed dried red chilli, 1 bay leaf, ½ crushed cinnamon stick, ½ tablespoon cardamom pods, and 2 crushed garlic cloves. Pour the vinegar into a pan, add the spice bag, and boil for 10 minutes. Set the pan aside and allow to cool before removing the spice bag. Strain the vinegar through a sieve into a jug once cool.

SOAK IN BRINE

Make the brine by dissolving the salt in 600ml (1 pint) of water in a large glass, or ceramic bowl. Stir well to dissolve until no salt crystals are visible. Add the vegetables, cover with a plate to keep them submerged, and leave to stand overnight at room temperature.

Tip If the prepared vegetables together weigh more than 500g (1lb 2oz) and you need more brine, use a ratio of 10g (⅓oz) salt to 100ml (3½fl oz) of water.

Mix the vinegar, coriander seeds, and mustard seeds in a jug, and leave to one side.

PACK INTO JARS

Wash the vegetables in water to rinse off the salt, drain, and dry on kitchen paper. Layer in a sterilized jar and pour over the spiced vinegar mix to cover the vegetables completely. Seal with a non-metallic or vinegar-proof lid and label. Leave at room temperature for 2 days, then chill in the fridge for at least 1 week before opening. Once opened, keep refrigerated.

Red Cabbage Pickle

**2 small
jars**

**1 day, plus
5–6 weeks**

**3 months,
refrigerated**

Ingredients

675g (1½lb) red cabbage, cored and shredded

1 red onion, sliced

3 tbsp sea salt

600ml (1 pint) white wine vinegar

125g (4½oz) light muscovado or caster sugar

1 tsp mustard seeds

1 tsp coriander seeds

SALT THE CABBAGE

Mix the cabbage, onion, and salt in a large glass or ceramic bowl until the vegetables are coated in salt. Transfer to a colander set over a bowl and place a plate inside the colander to weigh down the ingredients. Leave overnight at room temperature.

Why? The salt removes the moisture from the cabbage leaves. The plate helps to bring more of the leaves' surface into contact with the salt.

MAKE THE VINEGAR MIX

Pour the vinegar into a large jug, add the sugar and spices, and mix with a whisk to dissolve the sugar. Cover and leave overnight.

PREPARE THE VEGETABLES

Rinse the salt off the vegetables in cold running water. Drain and dry thoroughly with kitchen paper. The vegetables need to be completely dry to avoid diluting the vinegar.

PACK THE JARS

Pack the vegetables into sterilized jars. Stir the vinegar mix and pour it over the vegetables to completely cover them. Seal with non-metallic or vinegar-proof lids, label, and store in a cool, dark place for 1 week. Transfer to the fridge and store for 1 month for the flavours to mature. Once opened, keep refrigerated.

Careful! Make sure the vegetables are completely covered by the vinegar mix so that they are not exposed to airborne microbes.

Piccalilli

3 medium jars · **1 day, plus 1 month** · **6 months**

Ingredients

60g (2oz) sea salt

1 large cauliflower, cut into florets

2 large onions, peeled, quartered, and sliced finely, or use pickling onions

900g (2lb) mixed vegetables, such as courgettes, runner beans, carrots, green beans, cut into bite-sized pieces

2 tbsp flour

225g (8oz) granulated sugar

1 tbsp turmeric

60g (2oz) English mustard powder

900ml (1½ pints) ready-spiced pickling vinegar (see p.59)

SOAK IN BRINE

Put the salt and 1.2 litres (2 pints) water in a large glass or ceramic bowl and mix well. Add the vegetables, cover with a plate to keep them submerged, and leave to stand overnight at room temperature.

BLANCH THE VEGETABLES

Wash the vegetables to rinse off the brine. Bring a large pan of water to the boil, add half of the vegetables, and blanch for about 2 minutes. Drain and immediately dip the vegetables in cold water to halt the cooking process. Repeat with the rest of the vegetables. It's important to keep the batches small, so as not to overcrowd the pan. The blanching process only begins when the water returns to the boil.

Tip Cook the vegetables until they are just *al dente* and still crunchy; don't overcook them.

MAKE THE SPICED VINEGAR SAUCE

Form a spice paste by putting the flour, sugar, turmeric powder, and mustard powder in a small bowl and mixing with a little vinegar. Transfer to a large stainless-steel saucepan, pour in the rest of the vinegar, and bring to the boil, stirring constantly.

Why? Mixing the ingredients into a paste binds them together. As you add the vinegar it dilutes the ingredients to a loose paste and then a smooth sauce. Stirring the sauce continuously ensures the ingredients won't subsequently separate and form lumps.

Simmer the spiced vinegar for 15 minutes, then remove from the heat. Add the vegetables to the pan, stir until they are well coated in the sauce, and ladle into sterilized jars. Seal with non-metallic or vinegar-proof lids, label, and store in a cool, dark place for at least 1 month for the flavours to mature. Once opened, keep refrigerated.

Tip Press the piccalilli down as you fill the jars to remove any air pockets. This will ensure that no airborne microbes in the trapped air bubbles come into contact with the food and spoil it.

How to **Make Freezer Pickles**

Freezer pickles don't need the same quantities of vinegar, salt, and
sugar as traditional pickles to preserve them; the freezing process
acts as an effective preservative. It also helps to retain the vegetables'
colour, flavour, and crunch. The vinegar, salt, and sugar are added to
provide the familiar taste of a pickle.

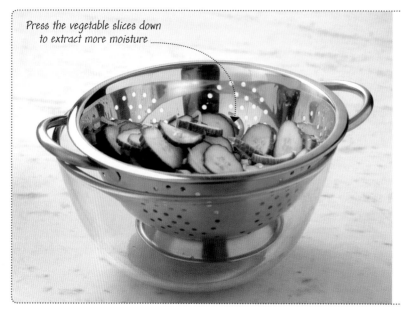

*Press the vegetable slices down
to extract more moisture* ....

Salting

Sprinkle salt over the
vegetable slices and leave
for 2 hours to extract their
moisture. This helps
retain their texture when
frozen and once thawed.
Rinse off the salt, to avoid
making the slices too
salty, drain well, and pat
dry to remove the last of
the moisture.

Pickling

Pour a solution of vinegar,
sugar, and spices over the
vegetables and refrigerate
overnight so the flavours
can mature. There's no
need to completely cover
the vegetables; freezing
will provide the sterile,
airless environment
traditionally provided by
the vinegar.

*The vinegar solution acts
like a marinade or
acidifier rather than a
sealant that excludes air.*

Bread and Butter Freezer Pickle

350–450g   **2¼ hours**   **6 months**
(12oz–1lb)

Ingredients

2 large cucumbers, scrubbed and sliced thinly

2 shallots, very finely sliced

½ green pepper, finely chopped (optional)

1–2 tsp sea salt

120ml (4fl oz) cider or wine vinegar

30–60g (1–2oz) caster sugar

a good pinch of ground turmeric

a good pinch of celery or dill seeds,
    or ½–1 tsp mustard seeds

SALT THE VEGETABLES

Mix the cucumbers, shallots, pepper (if using), and salt in a large glass or ceramic bowl until the vegetables are completely coated in salt. Leave for 2 hours at room temperature.

Remember The salt will draw moisture from the vegetables.

PREPARE THE VEGETABLES

Transfer the vegetables to a colander and wash to rinse off the salt. Drain well, pressing them down lightly with your hand to extract the moisture. Transfer to a dry bowl.

MARINATE IN THE SPICED VINEGAR

Mix the vinegar and sugar to taste, stirring to dissolve the sugar. Add the spices, and pour the spiced vinegar over the vegetables. Cover with a plate and marinate overnight in the fridge to develop a classic pickle flavour before being frozen.

Why? It's important to marinate before freezing because the flavours won't deepen and mingle once the pickle is frozen.

Tip If you like a sharp pickle, add less salt. For a milder pickle add more sugar.

POT UP IN A JAR

Divide the pickle between portion-sized freezer pots, leaving 1cm (½in) of space at the top to allow for expansion. Seal, label, date, and freeze. To use, thaw it in the fridge overnight first, then keep it refrigerated and consume within 1 week.

How to **Make Chutney**

Chutneys are versatile sweet-sour mixtures of vegetables, fruits, spices, and dried fruits, which are cooked slowly in vinegar, salt, and sugar to preserve them effectively. The heat produced as the chutney cooks also helps kill most microbes. There are only a couple of simple guidelines to follow to make this tasty savoury preserve with a bite!

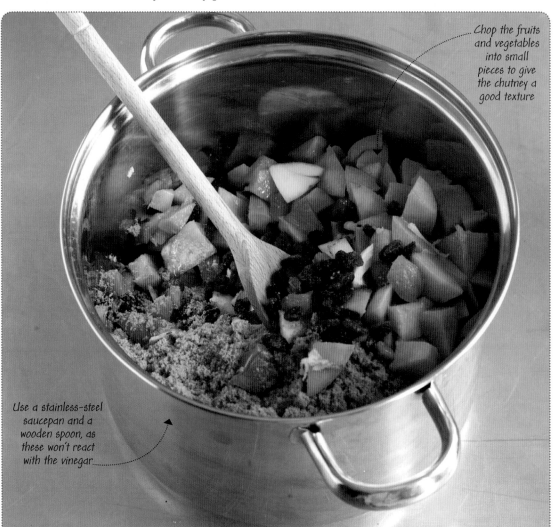

Chop the fruits and vegetables into small pieces to give the chutney a good texture

Use a stainless-steel saucepan and a wooden spoon, as these won't react with the vinegar

Cook the mixture slowly

Slow-cooking is the golden rule. Stir the chopped fruit, vegetables, spices, sugar, and vinegar mixture occasionally as it cooks. But as it thickens stir more frequently so it doesn't stick to the bottom of the pan and burn, which would give the chutney a burnt, bitter flavour.

Tip Sugar is a vital ingredient in any chutney, as it prevents the flesh and skins of fruits and vegetables softening too much and turning mushy. It's important to dissolve the sugar before you bring the mixture to the boil.

Reduce until the liquid has evaporated and the sugar and vinegar are at the optimum concentrations for preserving

The colours of the ingredients darken and the flavours intensify as the chutney cooks

Testing

Draw a wooden spoon across the base of the pan. If it leaves a clear trail for a few seconds, the chutney is ready. If lots of liquid covers the trail immediately, cook the chutney a little longer and keep testing it. Once potted up, let it mature for at least 1 month before consuming.

Practise MAKING CHUTNEY

Plum Chutney

The secret of deliciously tangy chutney is time: a long,
gentle cooking time, and then time for it to mature before
being opened. This basic recipe is ideal for all kinds of
seasonal produce, so experiment with different fruits and
vegetables – just keep the overall quantities the same.

3 large jars **Approx. 2 hours, plus 1–2 months** **12 months**

 plums
 cooking apples
 onions

Ingredients

1kg (2¼lb) plums

350g (12oz) cooking apples

250g (9oz) onions

125g (4½oz) raisins

300g (10½oz) light brown soft sugar

1 tsp sea salt

1 tsp each allspice, cinnamon, and coriander, freshly ground if possible

1 dried chilli or ½ tsp dried chilli flakes

1 tsp fennel seeds (optional)

600ml (1 pint) white wine or cider vinegar

 raisins
 light brown soft sugar
 sea salt
 spices

 dried chilli flakes

 fennel seeds

 sharp knife

 chopping board

 white wine vinegar

Equipment

sharp chopping knife

chopping board

stainless steel preserving pan or large, heavy-based stainless steel saucepan

large wooden spoon

wide-mouthed jam funnel

ladle

jars with vinegar-proof lids, or with cellophane covers and elastic bands

discs of waxed paper

 preserving pan

 wooden spoon

 wide-mouthed jam funnel

 ladle

 jars

discs of waxed paper and cellophane covers

67

1 Peel and finely slice the onions. Halve the plums, remove their stones, and cut the fruit into quarters. Core, peel, and roughly dice the cooking apples into bite-sized pieces.

Tip You can use slightly overripe or slightly imperfect produce, but carefully cut out and discard any bruised or damaged parts. The quality of the chutney depends on this kind of meticulous approach.

Chop the ingredients into small, evenly sized pieces so the chutney will have a good texture and a spoonable consistency

Use a wooden spoon to stir the mixture until the sugar has dissolved

2 Put all the ingredients into a preserving pan or a large heavy-based, stainless steel saucepan and bring slowly to the boil, stirring to dissolve the sugar.

Why? It's important to use a stainless steel pan and not a brass, copper, or iron pan, as these metals will react with the vinegar and give the finished chutney a metallic taste.

3 Turn the heat down and simmer gently for 1–1½ hours. Test the chutney by dragging a wooden spoon through the mixture along the base of the pan.

Careful! Make sure you stir the chutney frequently towards the end of the cooking time, so it doesn't catch and burn on the base of the pan.

The chutney is ready if a clear channel remains. It should have a thick, jam-like consistency and look glossy

Use a funnel to fill the sterilized jars with chutney

Stand the jars on a tray or board to catch any drips

Make sure there are no air pockets in the filled jars

4 Check the seasoning, add a little more salt if necessary, and pot into warm sterilized jars. Cover the hot chutney with discs of waxed paper and seal the jars.

Careful! Vinegar corrodes metal, so use plastic lids or metal lids that have a plastic seal or cover.

How to store

Store the sealed jars in a cool, dark place and leave to mature for 1–2 months. Chutneys can taste harsh and flat if eaten straight away.

Did anything go wrong?

The chutney has shrunk inside the jar. It has lost moisture, probably because the lid wasn't airtight. Make sure you seal each jar carefully.

Liquid has collected at the top of the jar. The chutney wasn't cooked for long enough. Cook it gently until the liquid evaporates.

The chutney has started to ferment. The vinegar solution was too weak, the storage conditions are too warm, or the chutney wasn't cooked long enough. Discard the chutney.

There is mould and an unpleasant odour. The chutney may have been contaminated; discard the chutney and sterilize all your equipment.

Try more Chutney recipes ▶ ▶ ▶

Runner Bean and Courgette Chutney

 3 medium jars

 2 hours

 9 months

Ingredients

600g (1lb 5oz) runner beans, thinly sliced

4 courgettes, thinly sliced

350g (12oz) cooking apples, peeled, cored, and chopped

2 onions, finely chopped

450g (1lb) light soft brown sugar

1 tsp mustard powder

1 tsp turmeric

1 tsp coriander seeds

600ml (1 pint) cider vinegar

COOK THE INGREDIENTS

Put all the ingredients in a preserving pan or large, heavy-based, stainless-steel saucepan. Cook over a gentle heat, stirring until the sugar has dissolved. Bring to the boil and cook at a rolling boil for 10 minutes, stirring occasionally. Then reduce the heat and simmer the mixture gently for about 1½ hours.

Careful! Stir continuously towards the end of the cooking time to prevent the mixture from sticking and burning on the base of the pan.

LADLE INTO JARS

Test whether the chutney is ready by drawing a spoon across the base of the pan to see if it leaves a clear trail. Ladle into sterilized jars. Cover with a waxed paper disc to stop any microorganisms coming into contact with the preserve and to prevent it from drying out. Place the disc wax-side down. Seal with non-metallic or vinegar-proof lids. Label and store in a cool, dark place for at least 1 month for the flavours to mature and mellow. Once opened, keep refrigerated.

Tip Press the chutney down as you fill the jars to remove any air pockets where microbes can grow.

Tomato and Roasted Pepper Chutney

3 medium jars | 2 hours 20 minutes | 9 months

Ingredients

1 red pepper

1 orange pepper

1 yellow pepper

1.35kg (3lb) ripe tomatoes

2 onions, roughly chopped

450g (1lb) granulated sugar

600ml (1 pint) white wine vinegar

PREPARE THE PEPPERS

Preheat the oven to 200°C (400°F/Gas 6). Arrange the peppers on a baking tray and roast for 25–30 minutes until they are slightly charred. Meanwhile, prepare the tomatoes by plunging them into boiling water for 1 minute and then peeling. When the peppers are cooked and still hot, put them in a plastic bag and leave to cool. Once cool, take the peppers out of the plastic bag and simply pull off the skins with your fingers and discard. Deseed, remove the stalks, and chop the flesh roughly.

Why? Cooling the peppers in a plastic bag creates condensation and makes them easy to peel.

CHOP THE VEGETABLES

Put the peeled tomatoes, chopped peppers, and onions in a food processor and blitz briefly until chopped but not mushy. Alternatively, chop the vegetables by hand.

COOK THE INGREDIENTS

Put all the ingredients in a preserving pan or large, heavy-based, stainless-steel saucepan. Cook over a gentle heat, stirring until the sugar has dissolved. Bring to the boil, then reduce the

heat and simmer the mixture gently for about 1½ hours, until it thickens to a jam-like texture.

Careful! Stir continuously towards the end so the mixture does not catch on the base of the pan and burn.

LADLE INTO JARS

Test whether the chutney is ready by drawing a spoon across the base of the pan to see if it leaves a clear trail. Ladle into sterilized jars making sure that there are no air pockets where mircoorganisms can thrive. Cover with a waxed paper disc and seal with non-metallic or vinegar-proof lids. Label and store in a cool, dark place, allowing the flavours to mature for at least 1 month. Once opened, keep refrigerated.

How to **Make Relish**

Part pickle, part chutney, relishes are crunchy, sweet-sour condiments of diced fruit and vegetables, sugar, and vinegar – often with a hint of spice. Relishes enhance any dish and are even easier to make than chutneys, as they are cooked for less time and are less concentrated – although this also means that they don't keep for as long.

To test, draw a spoon across the base of the pan to see that very little liquid is left

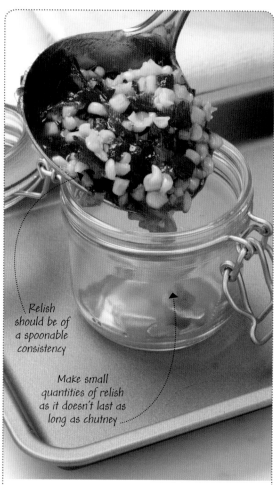

Relish should be of a spoonable consistency

Make small quantities of relish as it doesn't last as long as chutney

Cook gently

Dice the vegetables for a fine, spoonable texture. Put the ingredients in a large pan. Stir over a low heat to dissolve the sugar, and bring to the boil. Let it simmer for 15–20 minutes, stirring frequently, until it is slightly thick and most of the liquid has evaporated.

Potting up

When the relish is still quite wet, remove it from the heat and pot up into warm sterilized jars using a ladle. Seal the jars with non-metallic or vinegar-proof lids. Relish can be eaten immediately, but must be stored in the fridge once opened.

Sweetcorn and Pepper Relish

2 small jars

35–40 minutes

3 months

Ingredients

4 sweetcorn cobs

2 medium red peppers, or 1 green and
    1 red pepper, deseeded and finely diced

2 celery sticks, finely sliced

1 red chilli, deseeded and finely sliced (optional)

1 medium onion, finely sliced

450ml (15fl oz) white wine vinegar

225g (8oz) granulated sugar

2 tsp sea salt

2 tsp mustard powder

½ tsp ground turmeric

PREPARE THE SWEETCORN

Separate the kernels from the cobs by holding a cob upright in one hand and running a sharp knife down the sides to slice off the kernels. Bring a pan of water to the boil and blanch the sweetcorn kernels in the boiling water for 2 minutes. Drain well.

COOK THE INGREDIENTS

Put all the ingredients into a preserving pan or large, heavy-based, stainless-steel saucepan and heat the mixture, stirring to dissolve the sugar. Bring to the boil, turn the heat down, and simmer gently, stirring often, for 15–20 minutes.

POT UP THE RELISH

Test whether the relish is ready by drawing a spoon across the base of the pan. If just a little liquid is left, the relish is ready. Ladle into

sterilized jars. Cover with a waxed paper disc, seal with non-metallic or vinegar-proof lids, and label. Once opened, keep refrigerated.

Tip The relish goes well with burgers and barbecued meats and can be consumed immediately, though the flavours will improve after a few weeks in storage.

Spicy Carrot Relish

1 small jar   **Approx. 1 hour**   **3 months**

Ingredients

2 tsp coriander seeds

handful of cardamom pods

2.5cm (1in) piece of fresh root ginger

500g (1lb 2oz) carrots, grated

1 tsp mustard seeds

juice and zest of 1 orange

120ml (4fl oz) cider vinegar

125g (4½oz) granulated or light soft brown sugar

PREPARE THE SPICES

Crush the coriander seeds lightly in a pestle and mortar. Extract the cardamom seeds from the pod by lightly crushing with a pestle and then pulling the skin apart with your fingers. You need about 1 teaspoon of seeds. Peel the ginger using the edge of a teaspoon, then finely grate it.

COOK THE INGREDIENTS

Put the carrots and mustard, coriander, and cardamom seeds into a preserving pan or large, heavy-based saucepan and stir. Add the ginger, orange juice and zest, vinegar, and sugar and heat the mixture, stirring until the sugar dissolves. Cook gently for 10 minutes stirring often, to soften the carrots. Turn up the heat a little and let the mixture simmer, stirring frequently, for 15–20 minutes.

POT UP THE RELISH

Test whether the relish is ready by drawing a spoon across the pan's base to see if there is just a little liquid left. Ladle into sterilized jars. Cover with a waxed paper disc, seal with non-metallic or vinegar-proof lids, and label. Store in a cool, dark place for 1 month to let the flavours mature. Once opened, keep refrigerated. Goes well with curry.

Tomato Relish

1 medium jar   **1 hour 40 minutes**   **6 months**

Ingredients

1kg (2¼lb) ripe tomatoes, skinned if you prefer

2 onions, roughly chopped

3 courgettes, roughly chopped

1 yellow pepper, deseeded and roughly chopped

2 garlic cloves

2 red chillies, stalks removed (or more if you like it hot)

2 tbsp tomato purée

1 tsp English mustard powder

300ml (10fl oz) malt or cider vinegar

150g (5½oz) granulated sugar

CHOP THE VEGETABLES

Either chop the tomatoes, onions, courgettes, pepper, garlic, and chilli by hand or process in separate batches in a food processor. Whiz until chopped using the pulse button, taking care that the vegetables aren't chopped too fine.

COOK THE INGREDIENTS

Put the chopped vegetables in a preserving pan or a large heavy-based, stainless-steel saucepan. Stir in the tomato purée and mustard powder, then add the vinegar and sugar. Simmer, stirring continously, until the sugar has dissolved, then turn the heat up and cook steadily for 40 minutes–1 hour, stirring frequently, or until the mixture begins to thicken.

POT UP THE RELISH

Ladle into a warm sterilized jar with non-metallic or vinegar-proof lids, seal, and label. Store in a cool, dark place. Allow to mature for 1 month, and refrigerate after opening.

Beetroot Relish

 2 small jars   **2¼ hours**   **9 months**

Ingredients

1.35kg (3lb) raw beetroots

1 tsp caster sugar

450g (1lb) shallots, finely chopped

600ml (1 pint) cider or white wine vinegar

1 tbsp pickling spices, sealed in a muslin
bag (see p.57)

Special Equipment

small square of muslin and string

COOK THE BEETROOT

Put the beetroots and sugar in a preserving
pan or large heavy-based, stainless steel saucepan,
cover with water, and bring to the boil. Simmer
for 1 hour or until the beetroots are soft and
cooked. Drain and set aside to cool. Once cold,
peel and dice.

Careful! Beetroots can stain skin and clothes. If
you don't want your fingers to get stained, peel the
beetroot wearing clean rubber gloves.

COOK THE RELISH

Rinse out the pan, add the shallots and vinegar,
and cook on a low heat for 10 minutes. Add the
diced beetroots and the bag of pickling spices, stir
the mixture, and add the sugar. Stir until the sugar
has dissolved and bring to the boil. Cook at a rolling
boil for 5 minutes, then reduce the heat and simmer
the relish for 40 minutes or until it thickens.

POT UP THE RELISH

Draw a spoon across the base of the pan to see
if the relish is ready – there should be only a little
liquid left. Remove the spice bag and ladle into
sterilized jars. Cover with a waxed paper disc,
seal with non-metallic or vinegar-proof lids,
and label. Once opened, keep refrigerated.

Tip This relish is best stored in a cool, dark place
for 1 month to allow the flavours to mature fully,
although it can be eaten immediately. It goes well
with cheeses or beef.

2

Build On It

This chapter expands your knowledge of, and confidence in, preserving. It will allow you to really get stuck into some of the classic techniques for preserving fruit – such as jams and jellies – that tend to involve a little more skill than savoury preserves.

In this section, learn to prepare or make:

Fruit Cheese
pp.78–85

Jam
pp.86–97

Conserve
pp.98–101

Jelly
pp.102–109

Syrups and Cordials
pp.110–115

Fruits in Syrup
pp.116–123

Dried Fruit and Veg
pp.124–131

How to **Make Fruit Cheese**

Fruit cheese is a misleading name, as this preserve doesn't actually contain any dairy produce – or taste much like it – although it does go well with cheese! Fruit cheeses are intensely flavoured fruit purées, which have been cooked with sugar until they are concentrated, and are solid enough to slice once they cool. The related fruit butters are less intense, lightly sweetened purées with a spreadable texture.

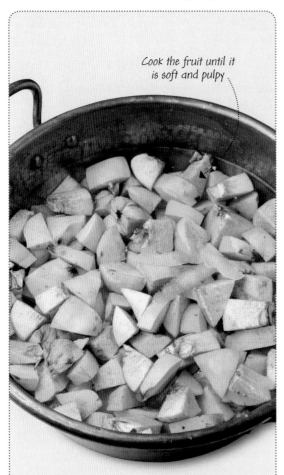

Cook the fruit until it is soft and pulpy

Use a measuring jug to calculate how much purée you have

Cook and sieve the fruit

Simmer chopped fruit with some water in a preserving pan or large saucepan until it turns to a pulp. Then pass the fruit pulp – in batches, if necessary – through a sieve or foodmill. Set the sieve over a large, clean bowl to collect the purée.

Measure the purée

Next, measure the purée so you know how much sugar has to be added. Spoon the purée into a measuring jug. You need 450g (1lb) of granulated sugar for every 450ml (15fl oz) of cooked, sieved fruit pulp that you measure.

Tip To make fruit butter, simply stop the cooking halfway through the slow-cooking process. At this point, the purée should be a thick, but not yet stiff, paste. It's ready when a spoon pressed down on it leaves a clear indent.

The sugar has dissolved when you can't feel any grittiness on the base of the pan

The paste should ooze slowly as you spoon or pour it into a mould

Reduce to paste

Put the purée in a clean pan and add the sugar. Cook over a low heat, stirring with a wooden spoon until the sugar dissolves. Bring to the boil, then turn the heat down and slow cook for the required amount of time, stirring occasionally.

Pour into moulds

The fruit cheese is ready when it looks dark, thick and glossy, sticks to the spoon, and leaves a trail if you draw the spoon across the base of the pan. When ready, pour the fruit cheese into greased sterilized moulds and leave to cool and set.

Membrillo

A traditional Spanish delicacy, often served with Manchego cheese, this lightly scented fruit cheese is made from quinces, which are cooked down into a thick, stiff paste. It has a concentrated flavour and keeps for a long time. Always use delicious fruit in prime condition for this versatile preserve.

6 ramekin dishes **1½ hours** **12 months or longer**

Ingredients

1kg (2¼lb) quinces, scrubbed

juice of ½ lemon

approx. 450g (1lb) granulated sugar

groundnut or sunflower oil, for greasing

Equipment

preserving pan or large, heavy-based saucepan

large wooden spoon

fine mesh sieve

large, clean bowl

measuring jug

ramekins or other ceramic moulds, or a shallow baking tray

baking parchment and string (optional)

quinces

lemon juice

granulated sugar

preserving pan

wooden spoon

sieve

bowl

measuring jug

ramekin

1 Put the chopped quinces in a preserving pan or a large heavy-based saucepan with 600ml (1 pint) of water and the lemon juice. Bring to the boil and simmer for 30 minutes, and when the fruit is soft, lightly crush with a potato masher or fork.

Remember There is no need to peel or core the quinces before you chop them, as you will be sieving the cooked fruit.

Scrape down the underside of the sieve after each batch, before discarding the waste pulp

2 Remove the pan from the heat and leave to cool slightly. Then sieve the pulp in batches over a large, clean bowl. Measure the purée: for every 450ml (15fl oz) of purée, add 450g (1lb) of sugar.

Tip Press the pulp hard against the side of the fine mesh sieve with a wooden spoon to extract as much of the purée as possible.

3 Put the purée back in the pan, add the sugar, and stir over a low heat to dissolve the sugar. Bring to the boil, then simmer gently for 45–60 minutes, stirring only occasionally at first.

Careful! Start stirring the purée more regularly towards the end of the cooking time, so it does not catch and burn on the base of the pan.

The mix will bubble and spit, so take care

4 Test the paste to see if it is ready by dragging a wooden spoon across the base of the pan. The paste should leave a trail, look stiff and glossy, and stick to the spoon when it is ready.

Tip For extra taste, you can add unusual flavourings, such as rosewater or aromatic liqueurs, near the end of the cooking time, before you pour the paste into moulds.

Stir the mixture often, especially near the end of the cooking time

The fruit cheese will turn solid as it cools

5 Lightly grease warm, sterilized ramekin dishes or moulds with a little oil. Spoon in the paste, level the top, and leave it to cool. To store, seal the moulds with waxed paper discs and cellophane.

Tip If you want to reuse the ramekins once the membrillo has cooled, loosen the moulds with a palette knife, turn out the membrillo, and wrap each of the blocks in parchment and tie with string.

How to store

Membrillo can be stored for 12 months or longer. When you need it, turn it out of the mould (or unwrap it) and slice it finely.

Store all fruit cheeses in a cool, dark place for at least 4–6 weeks to mature in flavour.

Try other fruit

Other good fruits for fruit cheeses and butters include plums, damsons, pears, apples (combined with quinces or damsons for a fruit cheese), boysenberries, grapes, greengages, loganberries, medlars, mulberries, and tayberries.

Try more Fruit Cheese recipes ▶ ▶ ▶

Damson Cheese

3 ramekin dishes   **2–2½ hours**   **2 years**

Ingredients

1kg (2¼lb) damsons, stoned and roughly chopped

granulated sugar (see method)

15–30g (½–1oz) butter (optional)

MAKE A PURÉE

Simmer the fruit in a preserving pan or large, heavy-based saucepan with 300ml (10fl oz) of water for 30–40 minutes until it is a thick pulp. Crush the fruit with the back of a fork or potato crusher as it cooks. Pour the pulp into a fine sieve held over a bowl and collect the juice and purée.

Pour the purée into a measuring jug and add the sugar. For every 600ml (1 pint) of purée add 450g (1lb) of sugar. Taste the purée and if it seems a little sharp, mix in an additional 150g (5¼oz) of sugar per 600ml (1 pint) of purée. Put the purée, sugar, and butter, if using, back in the pan, stir over a low heat to dissolve the sugar, and slowly bring to the boil.

Tip Adding butter helps to soften and mellow the sharp flavour of the damsons.

COOK GENTLY

Simmer the purée gently for 35–45 minutes, or longer, stirring often, until it forms a glossy paste and "plops".

Careful! Stir regularly to ensure the purée doesn't catch and burn on the base of the pan.

Test whether the cheese is ready by drawing a spoon across the base of the pan to see if it leaves a clear trail.

FILL AND STORE

Oil 3 ramekin dishes lightly and fill with the cheese. Either cover with waxed paper discs and cellophane or leave to cool, turn out of the moulds, and wrap in waxed paper or cling film. Label and store in a cool, dark place for at least 6–8 weeks to mature. Damson cheese works well sliced with cold meats and cheeses or as an after-dinner sweetmeat.

Apple Butter

3 medium
jars

2 hours
25 minutes

6 months

Ingredients

900g (2lb) cooking apples, roughly chopped

juice of 1 orange

pinch of ground allspice

pinch of ground cinnamon

675g (1½lb) granulated sugar

MAKE A PURÉE

Simmer the apples in a preserving pan or large heavy-based saucepan with 250ml (8fl oz) water for 10 minutes until they are soft. Pour the fruit pulp into a fine sieve held over a bowl and collect the juice and purée.

COOK GENTLY

Put the purée back in the pan and add the orange juice, ground allspice, cinnamon, and sugar. Stir over a low heat to dissolve the sugar, and slowly bring to the boil. Simmer the purée gently for 2 hours or longer, stirring every so often so that it doesn't catch and burn on the base of the pan, until it thickens.

TEST THE BUTTER

The butter is ready when a spoon drawn across the base of the pan leaves a clear trail. The butter should also be thick enough to rest on the back of the spoon without running off.

POT UP IN JARS

Ladle into sterilized jars. Cover with waxed paper discs, seal, and label. Store in a cool, dark place. Once opened, keep refrigerated. Apple butter keeps for up to 6 months and goes well with good, fresh bread and in desserts.

How to **Make Jam**

Jam-making is a popular pursuit, and a skill that's immensely satisfying to learn. The concept is simple: fruit is preserved with sugar by cooking over a high heat until it sets. As the fruit cooks it releases the gum-like substance called pectin, which is a natural setting agent. For a good set the balance of sugar, pectin, and acid must be correct (see pp.88–89).

Soften the fruit and add sugar

The fruit is prepared according to the recipe and simmered in water until soft. Pour the sugar into the pan and stir with a wooden spoon until the sugar has completely dissolved.

Careful! Do not add the sugar until the fruit has cooked enough to become soft and release its pectin: sugar inhibits the release of pectin and toughens the fruit skins.

Dissolve the sugar over a low heat so the jam does not become grainy

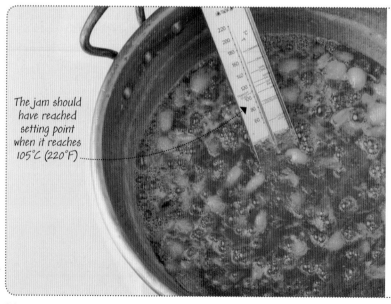

Boil rapidly

Turn the heat up high and bring the mixture to a rapid, rolling boil to give the pectin time to set with the sugar. Rapidly boiling jam rises in the pan and becomes frothy with masses of small bubbles; it should – theoretically – set when the sugar reaches 105°C (220°F). If you don't have a sugar thermometer, start testing for set when the bubbles become larger and start to "plop".

The jam should have reached setting point when it reaches 105°C (220°F)

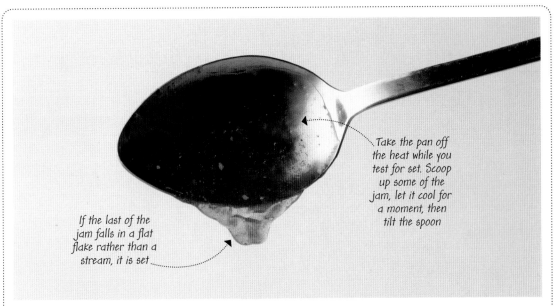

If the last of the jam falls in a flat flake rather than a stream, it is set

Take the pan off the heat while you test for set. Scoop up some of the jam, let it cool for a moment, then tilt the spoon

Flake test

To get rapid results when testing, place some saucers in the fridge to chill while you make the jam

Take the pan off the heat and put 1 teaspoon jam on the cold saucer. Let it cool, then push it to one side with your finger. If it wrinkles and your finger leaves a trail, it is set

Wrinkle test

Test for a set

Jam sets when it has been sufficiently cooked, typically between 5 and 20 minutes. Take the pan off the heat and test for set sooner rather than later: over-done jam is hard, rubbery, and difficult to salvage, but if jam is runny and not quite ready, continue boiling and test it again.

Understanding **Pectin and Acid in Fruit**

Jam forms when pectin – the gum-like substance released as the fruit simmers – reacts with sugar and acid to make a jelly. The natural acid found in fruit helps to release the pectin and avoid a lengthy cooking process (which might spoil the taste of the jam) while the sugar enables the pectin to gel. The crucial factor in achieving a jelly, or "set", is to have the right balance of pectin and acid.

*Sharp or tart tasting fruits, such as **crab apples**, tend to have higher acid content*

*Low-pectin fruits, such as **pears**, need extra pectin and acid to achieve a set.*

*High-pectin fruits, such as **redcurrants**, set easily to give a solid set, and absorb more sugar.*

*Medium-pectin fruits, such as **apricots**, set satisfactorily, usually giving a softer set.*

Adding extra acid

If the acid levels of a particular fruit are low (see table), add extra acid when you begin the cooking process to help the fruit release its pectin and achieve a set. The acid also helps to improve the colour and flavour of jam and prevent sugar crystallization. There are two ways to increase the acid levels:

Add lemon juice. Add the juice of 1 lemon (2 tablespoons) for every 1kg (2¼lb) fruit you use.

Add citric or tartaric acid, available from pharmacies. For every 1kg (2¼lb) fruit you use, add ½ teaspoon citric or tartaric acid dissolved in 4 tablespoons water.

Jam sugar

....Measure the liquid pectin out carefully

Liquid pectin

Powdered pectin

Adding extra pectin

There are several options for fruits that lack enough natural pectin to make a set, however if you need to add a lot of pectin you may have to adjust the amount of sugar in the recipe to compensate. Jam sugar is specially formulated to contain the correct balance of pectin and sugar. Powdered and liquid pectin is commercially available; mix powdered pectin into the sugar before you add to the fruit. Liquid pectin is very concentrated; follow the manufacturer's instructions.

Pectin and Acid Content of Key Fruits

For the best results choose slightly under-ripe fruit for jam-making because pectin levels tend to decrease as fruit ages. The riper the fruit, the less pectin it's likely to contain.

Fruits	Pectin content	Acidity
Blackcurrants	High	High
Crab apples	High	High
Cranberries (unripe)	High	Medium
Gooseberries	High	High
Plums (unripe), damsons	High	High
Quinces	High	High–medium
Red- and white currants	High	High
Citrus fruits (pectin is found in the skins, peel, and pith)	High–medium	High–medium
Cooking apples	High–medium	High–medium
Apricots	Medium	Medium
Cranberries (ripe)	Medium	Medium
Grapes (unripe) (variable pectin content)	Medium	Medium
Loganberries	Medium	Medium
Medlars	Medium	Low
Morello (cooking) cherries	Medium	Medium
All plums (ripe)	Medium	Medium
Raspberries	Medium	Medium
Blackberries	Low–medium	Low
Blueberries (variable pectin content)	Low–medium	Low
Wild blackberries (brambles)	Low	Low
Cherries (dessert)	Low	Low
Figs	Low	Low
Grapes (ripe) (variable pectin content)	Low	Low
Melons	Low	Low
Nectarines	Low	Low
Peaches	Low	Low
Pears	Low	Low
Rhubarb	Low	High
Strawberries	Low	Low

Practise MAKING JAM

Raspberry Jam

Home-made jam has a delicious depth of flavour
and fruity freshness that you don't find in shop-bought
produce. This straightforward recipe produces a lovely
soft-set raspberry jam, and is also suitable to
use with other soft-skinned berries.

2 small jars **25–30 minutes** **6 months**

Ingredients

650g (1½lb) raspberries
 (preferably not overripe)

juice of ½ lemon

500g (1lb 2oz) granulated sugar

raspberries

lemon juice

granulated sugar

Equipment

preserving pan or large,
 heavy-based saucepan

large wooden spoon

sugar thermometer (optional)

sterilized wide-mouthed jam
 funnel (optional)

ladle

skimmer or slotted spoon (optional)

sterilized jars with metal lids or
 cellophane covers and elastic bands

discs of waxed paper

preserving pan

wooden spoon

sugar thermometer

wide-mouthed jam funnel

ladle

slotted spoon

jars

elastic bands

discs of waxed paper and cellophane covers

1 Put a few small saucers in the fridge to chill. Place the fruit in a preserving pan or large heavy-based saucepan. Add the lemon juice and 150ml (5fl oz) of water. The lemon juice provides extra acid, which is vital for setting, as raspberries tend to be low in acid.

Tip Ensure the berries are in perfect condition and use soon after picking. Wash them only if they need it, as dry fruit is best.

Raspberries that aren't overripe are best for making jam

Keep the heat low until the sugar has completely dissolved

2 Simmer the fruit gently for 3–5 minutes to soften and release its juices. Then add the sugar and stir it in over a gentle heat. Once it has all dissolved, turn the heat to high.

Remember Sugar inhibits the release of pectin and toughens the skins of fruits, so always add it to the pan after the fruit has softened sufficiently.

3 Bring the jam to a rolling boil for 5–10 minutes or until the setting point is reached. Start testing for the setting point when the bubbles in the jam become large and start "plopping".

Help! If you are worried about missing the setting point, it is better to test early and frequently than wait too long before testing.

Push the jam to one side with your finger to see if it wrinkles slightly

4 Take the pan off the heat to test for a set. If you are doing a wrinkle test (see p.87), use one of the cold saucers placed in the fridge earlier.

Tip If you want to double-check the jam is set, use a flake test: put a little jam in a bowl, scoop up some with a spoon, let it cool for a moment, and tilt the spoon. If the last of the jam falls in a flat flake rather than a stream, it is set.

5 Ladle the jam into warm sterilized jars (see p.11) using a sterilized jam funnel. Fill the jars almost to the brim. Cover the hot jam with waxed paper discs and seal with metal lids, or cellophane covers and elastic bands.

Help! If there is scum on the surface of the jam, use a skimmer to remove it before you pot up, or stir the jam in the same direction until the scum has dispersed.

Jam funnels have wide mouths and brims to catch any drips

How to store

Label and store your batches of jam in a cool, dark place. They will keep for about 6–9 months. Refrigerate after opening; use within 3–4 weeks.

Did anything go wrong?

The jam won't set. It is under-boiled or too low in pectin. Try boiling it again briefly with commercial pectin. If it still doesn't set, re-boil with lemon juice.

The jam is flavourless, dull, and hard. It is over-boiled. Start testing sooner next time, and always turn off the heat while you test for a set.

The jam has fermented. You may have used overripe fruit, not used enough sugar, not sealed it properly, or stored the jam in too warm a place.

The jam has crystallized. You may have added too much sugar, stored the jars in too cold a place, or you may need more acid – add 2 tablespoons of lemon juice for every 1kg (2¼lb).

Try more Jam recipes ▶ ▶ ▶

Plum Jam with Spiced Port

6 medium jars   **45 minutes**   **9 months**

Ingredients

1.8kg (4lb) dark plums, stoned
    and cut into quarters

1 cinnamon stick, snapped in half

juice of 1 lime

1.35kg (3lb) granulated sugar

2–3 tbsp port, to taste

Place 1 or 2 plates in the fridge or freezer to chill.

SIMMER THE FRUIT

Put the plums, cinnamon, and lime juice into a preserving pan or a large, heavy-based saucepan, then pour over 600ml (1 pint) of water.

Why? Plums are very high in pectin and can set very quickly to a solid mass. Adding water to the fruit dilutes the pectin to a more manageable level.

Place the pan over a medium heat and bring the fruit mix up to simmering point. Turn the heat down to low just as it starts to bubble, then simmer gently for 15–20 minutes or until the plums begin to break down and soften.

Remember For the freshest jam, you don't want the fruit to boil strongly at this stage, but simply to break it down to release the pectin.

BOIL TO A SET

Add the sugar to the fruit and stir with a wooden spoon until the sugar has completely dissolved. Turn the heat up high, bring to the boil, and keep at a rolling boil for 5–8 minutes or until the mixture thickens and the bubbles become large and start "plopping".

Test for a set using the wrinkle test. Take the pan off the heat. Place a teaspoon of the fruit mix on a chilled plate. Wait for a minute, then push it with your finger. If it offers resistance and wrinkles as you push it, the jam has reached the setting point. If the jam hasn't set, bring it back to a rolling boil for another minute and test again. Repeat as required.

POT UP THE JAM

When the jam has set, carefully remove the cinnamon sticks, stir in the port, then ladle the jam into warm sterilized jars. Cover with waxed paper discs, seal, and leave to cool. Label and store in a cool, dark place and refrigerate after opening.

Help! If the potted jam does not cool to a set, all is not lost: simply tip out into a pan, bring back to a rolling boil for 1–2 minutes, and test again.

Blackcurrant Jam

2 small jars

45 minutes

6–9 months

Ingredients

500g (1lb 2oz) blackcurrants, washed

675g (1½lb) granulated sugar

juice of 1 lemon

Place 1 or 2 plates in the fridge or freezer to chill.

SIMMER THE FRUIT

Put the blackcurrants in a preserving pan or heavy saucepan and pour in 450ml (15fl oz) of water. Put the pan on a low heat and simmer the fruit gently for 15–20 minutes.

Why? Blackcurrants have tougher skins than many other fruits, so simmering them in water first helps to soften their skins.

BOIL TO A SET

Add the sugar and lemon juice to the pan and stir the mixture until all the sugar has dissolved – there should be no sugar crystals visible as you stir. Turn the heat up high, bring to the boil, and keep at a rapid, rolling boil for 8–10 minutes or until the mixture thickens and the bubbles become large and start "plopping".

Test for a set using the wrinkle test. Take the pan off the heat. Place a teaspoon of the fruit mixture on a chilled plate. Wait for a minute, then push it with your finger. If it offers resistance and wrinkles as you push it, the jam has reached the setting point. If the jam hasn't set, bring it back to a rolling boil for 1 more minute and test again.

Tip Blackcurrants are high in both acid and pectin, so this jam should set quite easily and quickly.

POT UP THE JAM

When you have a set, ladle the jam into sterilized jars. Cover with discs of waxed paper, seal, and label. Store in a cool, dark place. Once opened, keep refrigerated.

Cherry Jam

3 medium jars

45 minutes

9 months

Ingredients

500g (1lb 2oz) cherries, stones removed and reserved

juice of 2 lemons

500g (1lb 2oz) jam sugar or granulated sugar mixed with 1 sachet powdered pectin

2 tbsp brandy or cherry brandy

Place 1 or 2 plates in the fridge or freezer to chill.

SIMMER THE FRUIT

Place the cherry stones in a square of muslin, gather into a bag and tie with string. Make sure the string is long enough to allow easy removal of the bag. Put the cherries along with the bag of stones into a preserving pan or a large, heavy-based saucepan.

Why? You needn't include the cherry stones, but they will add a subtle almond flavour to the jam.

Pour over 300ml (10fl oz) water. Place the pan over a medium heat. Bring to the boil, then reduce to a simmer and cook gently for 10–15 minutes or until the cherries are tender and begin to soften. Remove the bag of stones. Pour in the lemon juice and add the sugar. Heat gently, stirring until the sugar dissolves. No sugar crystals should be visible.

Tip If you want some of the cherries to remain chunky in the jam, don't cook them for too long.

BOIL TO A SET

Turn the heat up high and bring to the boil. Keep at a steady rolling boil, stirring occasionally with a long wooden spoon, for 8–10 minutes or until it thickens.

Careful! The boiling fruit mix is liable to spit. Stir with a long wooden spoon to keep hands clear.

Test for a set using the wrinkle test. Remove the pan from the heat. Place a teaspoon of the fruit mix on a chilled plate. Wait for a minute and then push it with your finger. If it offers resistance and wrinkles as you push it, the jam has reached the setting point. If the jam hasn't set, bring back to a rolling boil for a further 1 minute and test again.

POT UP THE JAM

Stir in the brandy, then ladle into jars. Cover with discs of waxed paper, seal, label, and store in a cool, dark place. Refrigerate after opening.

Help! If the potted jam does not cool to a set, simply tip it out into a pan, bring back to a rolling boil for 1–2 minutes, and test again.

Cherry Vodka Jam variation Replace the brandy with the same amount of plain vodka.

Rhubarb, Pear, and Ginger Jam

3 medium jars

45 minutes

9 months

Ingredients

675g (1½lb) fresh rhubarb, trimmed, rinsed and chopped into 2.5cm (1in) pieces

2 pears, peeled, cored, and chopped

800g (1¾lb) granulated sugar

juice of 1 lemon

juice of ½ orange

2 small balls of stem ginger, finely chopped

Place 1 or 2 plates in the fridge or freezer to chill.

SIMMER THE FRUIT

Put the rhubarb and pears in a preserving pan or heavy saucepan and pour in the sugar. Put the pan on a low heat and add the lemon juice, orange juice, and stem ginger. Stir until all the sugar has dissolved. No sugar crystals should be visible.

BOIL TO A SET

Turn the heat up high, bring to the boil, and keep at a rapid, rolling boil for 15–20 minutes until the mixture in the pan thickens and reaches the setting point.

Test for a set using the wrinkle test. Take the pan off the heat. Place a teaspoon of the fruit mixture on a chilled plate. Wait for a minute, then push it with your finger. If it offers resistance and wrinkles as you push it, the jam has reached the setting point.

Remember If the jam hasn't set, bring it back to a rolling boil for another minute and test again.

POT UP THE JAM

When you have a set, ladle the jam into sterilized jars. Cover with discs of waxed paper, seal, and label. Store in a cool, dark place. Once opened, keep refrigerated.

Tip This jam will taste lovely in a pastry tart or spread as a filling in a sponge cake.

How to **Make Conserve**

Making conserve involves most of the same techniques as jam, with a couple of simple differences. One is that the fruit is steeped in sugar first to firm up its skin; as you are not aiming for a strong set this means you can use riper fruit with less pectin. Secondly, conserves are boiled more gently than jam and are left to cool and thicken a little before they are potted.

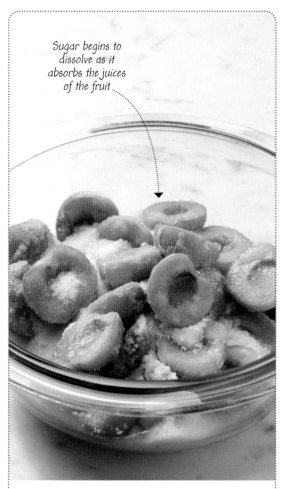

Sugar begins to dissolve as it absorbs the juices of the fruit...

Draw a spoon over the base of the pan: if it leaves a trail then the mixture has thickened sufficiently and you should test for a set...

Steep in sugar

The fruit is placed in a large bowl, coated with sugar, and allowed to steep. The sugar draws out the fruit juices, drying and firming the fruit. This firming stops the fruit from breaking down completely when boiled, leaving larger chunks of fruit in the conserve.

Allow to thicken

Conserves are cooked at a steady boil – not at the same rate and intense heat as for jam. Once the conserve has set, leave it to cool a little until it has thickened. The fruit will be more evenly distributed through the liquid, and is less likely to rise to the top of the jar.

Apricot Conserve

2 medium jars   30 minutes, plus steeping   6 months

Ingredients

500g (1lb 2oz) ripe apricots

350g (12oz) granulated sugar (or a little less, if you prefer a softer set and fresher taste)

juice of 1 lemon

Chill a couple of plates in the fridge or freezer so that they are ready for testing the set.

STEEP THE FRUIT IN SUGAR

Halve and stone the apricots, and layer them with the sugar in a bowl. Cover the bowl with a plate and leave for several hours or overnight at room temperature.

Remember It's worth spending this extra time preparing the fruit, as the sugar firms its flesh and and ensures the cooked conserve will contain large pieces of the fruit, for extra flavour and texture.

DISSOLVE THE SUGAR

Put the apricots and sugar with any juices in a preserving pan or heavy-based saucepan and add the lemon juice. Put the pan on a low heat and stir gently until all the sugar has dissolved.

Careful! Make sure you do not break up the fruit as you stir.

BOIL TO A SET

Turn the heat up high, bring to the boil, and keep it at a steady – not a rolling – boil for 7–10 minutes until the mix thickens and reaches the setting point. Avoid stirring the mix as you wait for a set. Take the pan off the heat and test for a set. Place a teaspoon of the mixture on a chilled plate. Wait 1 minute and then push it with your finger. If

it offers resistance and wrinkles as you push it, the mixture has set. If it does not wrinkle, bring it back to a steady boil for another minute and test again.

Remember For conserves you are looking to achieve a relatively soft set.

POT UP THE CONSERVE

Leave the conserve in the pan for a few minutes once you have a set, so the fruit can sink from the surface and distribute more evenly through the hot liquid. Then ladle the conserve into sterilized jars. Cover with discs of waxed paper, seal, and label. Store in a cool, dark place. All preserves, particularly ones that are made with a low amount of sugar, should be refrigerated once opened – they will all come into contact with the air when the lid is lifted.

Strawberry Conserve

3 medium jars   **45 minutes plus steeping**   **6 months**

Ingredients

900g (2lb) strawberries, hulled

900g (2lb) granulated sugar

juice of 1 lemon

juice of 1 lime

Special Equipment

muslin

Place 1 or 2 plates in the fridge or freezer.

STEEP THE FRUIT IN SUGAR

Layer the strawberries with the sugar in a bowl. Cover the bowl with a plate and leave for several hours or overnight at room temperature.

DISSOLVE THE SUGAR

Put the strawberries and sugar in a preserving pan or heavy-based saucepan, put the pan on a low heat, and stir gently until all the sugar has dissolved.

Careful! Try not to break up the fruit as you stir.

Boil the mix gently for about 5 minutes – just until the fruit has softened but not begun to break up. Remove the pan from the heat and cover loosely with muslin so the steam can escape and you aren't left with watery condensation. Set aside overnight.

BOIL TO A SET

Remove the muslin, stir in the lemon and lime juice, set the pan over a high heat, bring to the boil.

Why? Strawberries are low in pectin, and the citrus juices help to better release what pectin there is. The juices also provide a fresher flavour.

Boil the mixture at a steady boil, rather than rolling, for 5–10 minutes or until it thickens and reaches the setting point.

Tip Skim off any scum from the surface as the fruit boils so it doesn't affect the finished conserve.

Remove from the heat and test for the set. Place a teaspoon of the fruit mixture on a chilled plate. Wait for a minute, then push it with your finger. If it offers resistance and wrinkles as you push it, the setting point has been reached. If the mixture hasn't set, bring it back to a steady boil for 1 more minute and test again.

POT UP THE CONSERVE

Leave the conserve in the pan for a few minutes once you have a set so the fruit can sink from the surface and distribute more evenly through the hot liquid. Then ladle the conserve into sterilized jars. Cover with discs of waxed paper, seal, and label. Store in a cool, dark place. Once opened, keep refrigerated.

Peach and Walnut Conserve

3 medium jars | **45 minutes plus steeping** | **6 months**

Ingredients

1.25kg (2¾lb) ripe peaches

1 orange, peeled (but with pith still attached), and finely sliced

900g (2lb) granulated sugar

juice of 1 lemon

50g (2oz) walnuts, roughly chopped

1–2 tbsp brandy (optional)

Place 1 or 2 plates in the fridge or freezer.

PREPARE THE FRUIT

Lightly cut a cross on the top of each peach, drop it in a bowl of boiling water for 30 seconds, then transfer to a bowl of cold water. This helps to loosen the skin. Remove the peaches one by one and peel off the skin. Halve the peaches and remove and reserve all the peach stones. Roughly chop the flesh.

Tip Choose very ripe peaches, when their flavour and scent are at their best. You can also use ripe nectarines and prepare them in the same way.

STEEP THE FRUIT IN SUGAR

Layer the peaches, sliced orange, and sugar in a large bowl. Cover the bowl with a plate and leave for 4 hours or overnight at room temperature.

Why? Setting aside the uncooked fruit for this long enables the sugar to draw out the juices, which firms up the fruit and ensures it retains more of its form and texture in soft-set conserve.

DISSOLVE THE SUGAR

Tie the peach stones in a piece of muslin. Put the fruit and sugar in a preserving pan or heavy-based saucepan, add the bag of peach stones, then stir gently over a low heat until the sugar has dissolved.

BOIL TO A SET

Turn the heat up high, bring to the boil, and keep it at a steady boil, rather than rolling, for 15–20 minutes or until it thickens and reaches the setting point. Take the pan off the heat and test for a set. Place a teaspoon of the fruit mixture on a chilled plate. Wait for a minute, then push it with your finger. If it offers resistance and wrinkles as you push it, the setting point has been reached. If the mixture hasn't set, bring it back to a steady boil for 1 more minute and test again.

POT UP THE CONSERVE

Once you have a set, remove the bag of peach stones and stir in the lemon juice, walnuts, and brandy (if using). Leave the conserve in the pan for a few minutes so the fruit pieces can sink from the surface and distribute more evenly through the hot liquid. Then ladle the conserve into sterilized jars. Cover with discs of waxed paper, seal, and label. Store in a cool, dark place. Referigerate the conserve after opening.

How to **Make Jelly**

Bright, translucent, jewel-like jellies are sweet preserves made from
the strained juice of simmered fruit. They are prepared in the same
way as jams, with a couple of additional stages incorporated into
the process. An important point to remember when making jelly
is that the quantity of strained juice and pectin levels always vary.

Try fixing the jelly
bag to the legs of
an upturned stool
and set the bowl
underneath it

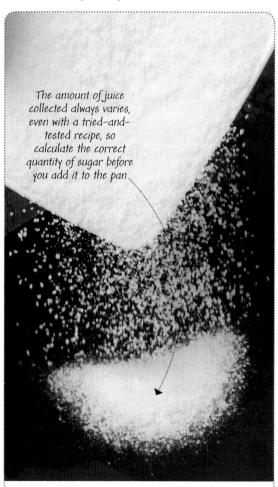

The amount of juice
collected always varies,
even with a tried-and-
tested recipe, so
calculate the correct
quantity of sugar before
you add it to the pan

Strain the fruit

Jellies are made by straining the juice of
simmered fruit through a jelly bag (or a clean
tea towel or a piece of muslin). For a clear
juice be patient and leave it to drip through
overnight. Resist the urge to squeeze the pulp,
which will make the juice and jelly cloudy.

Calculate and add sugar

The amount of sugar required depends
on the quantity of juice, which is different
every time. Use a measuring jug to check
what you collected and work out how much
sugar to add. The usual ratio is 450g (1lb)
of sugar for every 600ml (1 pint) of juice.

Wrinkle test

Flake test

Test the jelly

Boil and test the jelly mixture as you would to make jam. Take the pan off the heat while you test for a set (see p.87). For the wrinkle test, push some jelly with your finger to see if it wrinkles. For the flake test, tilt a spoonful of jelly to see if it falls in a flat flake.

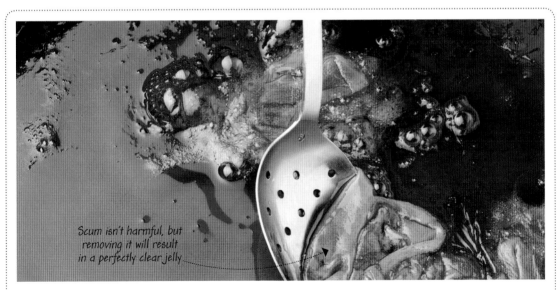

Scum isn't harmful, but removing it will result in a perfectly clear jelly

Skim off the scum

When the jelly reaches setting point, carefully skim off any bubbly scum caused by the vigorous boil. Make sure you don't accidently stir any of the froth into the boiling mixture. Keep a bowl of warm water nearby and rinse the skimmer every time you remove scum.

Grape, Lemon, and Clove Jelly

Fruits that are juicy or high in pectin – or preferably both –
make wonderful jellies. This recipe uses red grapes, which are
high in juice but have medium pectin levels, so the addition of
a lemon helps to produce a classic delicate jelly that sets well.
Like all jellies, it is delicious with cold meats or cheeses.

3 medium jars **1 hour plus straining** **12 months**

Ingredients

1.5kg (3lb 3oz) under-ripe red grapes (with pips), washed and chopped (see Tip, step 1)

1 lemon, washed and chopped

approx. 750g (1lb 10oz) granulated sugar (see method)

½ tsp cloves

red grapes

lemon

granulated sugar

cloves

Equipment

stainless steel preserving pan or large, heavy-based stainless steel saucepan

food processor (optional)

large wooden spoon

sterilized jelly bag or muslin-lined nylon sieve

sugar thermometer (optional)

wide-mouthed jam funnel (optional)

ladle

slotted spoon

sterilized jars with lids or with cellophane covers and elastic bands

discs of waxed paper

preserving pan

wooden spoon

jam funnel

elastic bands

jelly bag   **sugar thermometer**   **ladle**   **slotted spoon**   **jars**   **waxed paper and cellophane covers**

1 Put the grapes and the lemon in a preserving pan or large, heavy-based saucepan with 300ml (10fl oz) of water. Bring to the boil, cover, and cook gently for 35–40 minutes.

Tip If possible, use a food processor to chop the fruit. Finely chopped fruit requires less cooking time to soften before being strained. This results in a fruitier, fresher-tasting, clear jelly.

When the grapes soften, squash with a spoon to extract more juice

Boil-wash the jelly bag before using it so it is absolutely sterile

2 Strain the pulp through a jelly bag, or a clean nylon sieve lined with muslin, set over a large clean bowl. Leave to strain overnight, or for at least 2 hours, until no more juice drips through.

Careful! Don't squeeze the jelly bag or press the pulp to extract more juice, as it may cause your jelly to become cloudy.

3 Measure the strained juice and calculate the quantity of sugar: allow 450g (1lb) of sugar for every 600ml (1 pint) of juice.

Remember The quantity of juice always varies, so work out the amount of sugar required only after measuring the juice.

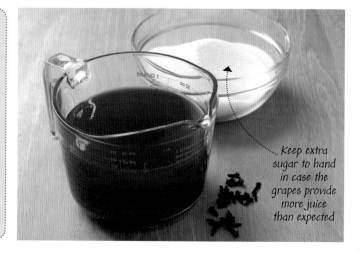

Keep extra sugar to hand in case the grapes provide more juice than expected

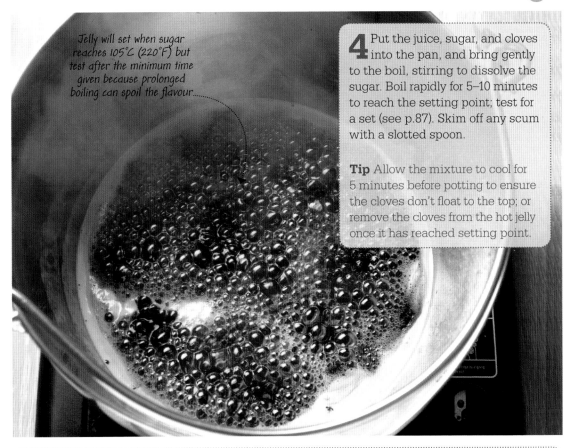

Jelly will set when sugar reaches 105°C (220°F) but test after the minimum time given because prolonged boiling can spoil the flavour.

4 Put the juice, sugar, and cloves into the pan, and bring gently to the boil, stirring to dissolve the sugar. Boil rapidly for 5–10 minutes to reach the setting point; test for a set (see p.87). Skim off any scum with a slotted spoon.

Tip Allow the mixture to cool for 5 minutes before potting to ensure the cloves don't float to the top; or remove the cloves from the hot jelly once it has reached setting point.

How to store

Pot into warm, sterilized jars, cover with waxed paper discs, and seal with metal lids, or use cellophane covers and elastic bands. Label and store your jars in a cool, dark place. They will keep for approximately 9–12 months.

Refrigerate opened jars of jelly and use within 3–4 weeks.

Did anything go wrong?

The jelly won't set, or turns very dark. You may have boiled it for too long. Prolonged boiling is detrimental to pectin and may mean the jelly will not set and will turn darker the longer it is boiled. The pectin content of fruit varies, so to ensure there is sufficient pectin to achieve a set, simmer the fruit with a chopped lemon and use jam sugar with added pectin (see p.89).

Try other fruits and combinations

Good choices include redcurrants; blackcurrants; strawberries – but add a chopped lemon because they vary in pectin; blackberries with apple and cinnamon; and quinces.

Apple jellies also make a good basis for herb jellies, such as rosemary and sage. Sour cooking apples have the most pectin.

Try more Jelly recipes ▶ ▶ ▶

Cranberry Jelly

2 small jars | **1¼ hours plus straining** | **6–9 months**

Ingredients

500g (1lb 2oz) fresh or frozen cranberries

1 tbsp lemon juice

approx. 500g (1lb 2oz) granulated sugar (see method)

Place 1 or 2 small plates in the fridge to chill.

EXTRACT THE JUICE

Put the berries in a preserving pan or large, heavy-based saucepan with 600ml (1 pint) water and the lemon juice. Put the pan on a medium heat and bring to the boil. Turn the heat down, cover, and simmer for 25–30 minutes until the cranberries are tender.

Mash the cooked berries with a fork or masher. Tip into a sterilized jelly bag, or muslin-lined sieve, set over a bowl and leave to strain overnight.

BOIL TO A SET

Measure the juice and work out the correct amount of sugar: allow 450g (1lb) of sugar for every 600ml (1 pint) of juice.

Why? You need to re-calcuate the sugar quantities each time you make the jelly because it's impossible to predict precisely how much juice the cranberries will yield.

Pour the juice into the preserving pan, add the sugar, and stir over a low heat until the sugar has dissolved. Turn the heat up high, bring to the boil, and keep it at a steady boil, rather than rolling, for 10–15 minutes until the mix thickens and reaches the setting point.

Take the pan off the heat and do a wrinkle test to check for a set. Place a teaspoon of the fruit

mixture on a chilled plate. Wait for a minute, then push it with your finger. If it offers resistance and wrinkles as you push it, the setting point has been reached. If the mixture hasn't set, bring it back to a rolling boil for 1 minute and test again.

POT UP THE JELLY

Skim off any scum that has formed on the surface when you have a set. Then ladle the jelly into sterilized jars. Cover with discs of waxed paper, seal, and label. Store in a cool, dark place. Once opened, refrigerate and eat within 3 weeks.

Rosemary Jelly

6 medium jars

1½ hours plus straining

9 months

Ingredients

a large handful of rosemary sprigs

900g (2lb) sour cooking apples, roughly chopped and with the core and pips retained

approx. 900g (2lb) granulated sugar (see method)

juice of 1 lemon)

Place 1 or 2 small plates in the fridge to chill.

OVEN-DRY THE ROSEMARY

Preheat the oven to 150°C (300F/Gas 2). Strip the rosemary leaves from their stalks and scatter onto a baking sheet. Reserve the stalks. Oven-dry the leaves for 30–40 minutes, then set aside to cool.

EXTRACT THE JUICE

Put the chopped apples, and their cores and pips, in a preserving pan or large, heavy-based saucepan with 1.2 litres (2 pints) of water. Add the rosemary stalks. Put the pan on a medium heat, bring to the boil, then simmer for 30–40 minutes until the apples are soft and mushy.

Why? Apple cores contain high levels of pectin to help achieve a good set and the rosemary stalks add flavour. Both can be added without affecting the texture of the jelly because the pulp is discarded after straining.

Break up the apples, if needed, with a fork or potato masher. Tip the pulp into a sterilized jelly bag, or a muslin-lined sieve, set over a bowl. Leave to strain, ideally overnight.

BOIL TO A SET

Measure the juice and calculate the sugar needed: allow 450g (1lb) of sugar for every 600ml (1 pint) of juice. Pour the juice, sugar, lemon juice,

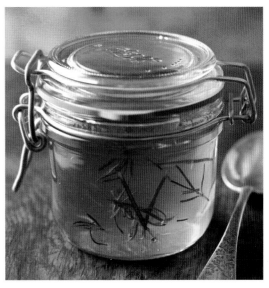

and oven-dried rosemary leaves in the pan and stir over a low heat until the sugar has dissolved.

Turn the heat up high, bring to the boil, and keep it at a rolling boil for 20 minutes until the juice thickens and reaches the setting point.

Take the pan off the heat and test for a set using the wrinkle test. Place a teaspoon of the fruit mixture on a chilled plate. Wait for a minute, then push it with your finger. If it offers resistance and wrinkles as you push it, the setting point has been reached. If the mixture hasn't set, bring it back to a rolling boil for 1 minute and test again.

POT UP THE JELLY

Skim off any scum that has formed on the surface when you have a set, and stir well.

Remember Leave the jelly for 10 minutes for the rosemary leaves to sink below the surface and distribute themselves evenly through the jelly.

Ladle into sterilized jars. Cover with discs of waxed paper, seal, and label. Store in a cool, dark place. Once opened, keep refrigerated and consume within 3 weeks.

How to **Make Syrups and Cordials**

Preserving seasonal produce as home-made syrups and cordials is
a wonderful way to enjoy the essence of its fruity flavours at any time
of year. The techniques of cooking the fruit, straining the juices, and
sweetening and preserving with sugar are easy to master.

*Use refined white
caster sugar so it
does not mask the
flavour of the juice*

*Check the quantity
of strained juice in
a measuring jug*

Simmer and strain the fruit

For the best flavour use minimal amounts of
water to simmer. Soft fruits like strawberries
only need a thin film, but for thick-skinned
fruits like blackcurrants use 150ml (5fl oz) of
water for every 450g (1lb) of fruit. Strain the
pulp, pressing gently to extract all the juice.

Sweeten the juice

Measure the juice to calculate the amount
of sugar. Every 500ml (16fl oz) of juice needs
350g (12oz) of sugar. Stir until the sugar has
dissolved, then add 1 teaspoon of citric acid
(vitamin C powder) to inhibit the growth of
bacteria and prevent discolouration.

Use a sterilized long-spouted funnel to bottle the sweetened juice

Use sterilized bottles with swing stopper lids for cordials and syrups

Tip Home-made syrups are extremely versatile ingredients. Dilute them with still or sparkling water to create refreshing drinks, or use them to add delicious flavours to ice creams, milkshakes, fruit salads, or smoothies.

Bottle the liquid

When the sugar has completely dissolved, pour the liquid immediately into warm sterilized bottles with the help of a sterilized funnel, or pour it into containers to freeze, leaving 2.5cm (1in) of space at the top of each container to allow for expansion.

Blackberry Syrup

2 small bottles   **25 minutes**   **1–2 months**

Ingredients

450g (1lb) ripe blackberries or loganberries

approx. 350g (12oz) caster sugar (see method)

1 tsp citric or ascorbic acid (vitamin C powder)

Special Equipment

large saucepan

sterilized jelly bag, or muslin and a fine sieve

mixing bowl

measuring jug

sterilized long-necked funnel

sterilized bottles

EXTRACT THE JUICE

Heat the blackberries in a saucepan with a little water – just enough to cover the base of the pan. Simmer over a gentle heat for a short time until the juices run, about 3–5 minutes. Crush the fruit with the back of a wooden spoon or a potato masher as it simmers.

Careful! Heat the fruit very gently over a low heat to preserve as much of the juice's nutritional content and flavour as possible.

STRAIN THE PULP

Transfer the pulp to a jelly bag or a muslin-lined sieve set over a bowl.

Careful! Press the pulp gently with a spoon to release the last of the juice. The gentle pressure ensures that the juice does not become clouded with pieces of pulp.

Pour the juice into a measuring jug and calculate the amount of sugar you will need. For every 500ml (16fl oz) of juice, use 350g (12oz) of sugar. Add the sugar and the citric acid to the juice and stir until the sugar has completely dissolved.

POUR INTO BOTTLES

When all the sugar has dissolved, pour the syrup into bottles using the funnel. Seal the bottles, leave to cool, label, and store in the fridge.

Remember If you want to keep the syrup for longer, you can pour it into freezer pots and store in the freezer for up to 6 months until you need it. Make sure you leave 2.5cm (1in) at the top of each pot for the liquid to expand as it freezes.

Strawberry Syrup

2 small bottles

25–35 minutes

1–2 months

Ingredients

450g (1lb) strawberries, hulled and sliced

1 tbsp lemon juice

1 vanilla pod, split, with seeds scraped out and reserved, or 1 tsp vanilla extract

200–250g (7–9oz) caster sugar (see method)

1 tsp citric or ascorbic acid (vitamin C powder)

Special Equipment

large saucepan

sterilized jelly bag, or muslin and a fine sieve

mixing bowl

measuring jug

sterilized long-necked funnel

sterilized bottles

EXTRACT THE JUICE

Heat the strawberries in a saucepan with approximately 200ml (7fl oz) water. Simmer over a gentle heat for a short time until the juices run. Crush the fruit with the back of a wooden spoon or a potato masher as it cooks.

Remember The delicate skins of strawberries willingly release their juice, so make sure you only just cover them with a film of water to avoid diluting the juice more than necessary, or losing too much flavour.

STRAIN THE PULP

Tip the pulp into a jelly bag or muslin-lined sieve set over a bowl. Press the pulp gently with a spoon to release the last of the juice.

Pour the juice into a measuring jug and work out how much sugar to use. For every 100ml (3½fl oz) of juice, use 70g (2½oz) of sugar.

COOK THE SYRUP

Clean out the pan and pour the juice back into it. Add the sugar and vanilla pod, and whisk in the vanilla seeds. Set the pan over a low heat and cook gently, without stirring, until the sugar has completely dissolved and the crystals are no longer visible. Bring to the boil and simmer for 5 minutes.

POUR INTO BOTTLES

Take the pan off the heat, remove the vanilla pod and discard, and stir in the citric acid. Pour the syrup into bottles using a funnel. Seal the bottles, leave to cool, label, then store in the fridge.

Serve with sliced strawberries – or if you're feeling decadent, try adding it to champagne or sparkling wine to make a dazzling aperitif.

Raspberry and Vanilla Syrup variation
Replace the strawberries with raspberries, use 250g (9oz) of caster sugar, and omit the lemon juice. There's no need to scrape out the vanilla seeds – just put the whole split pod into the juice and cook over a gentle heat without stirring until the sugar dissolves.

Fresh Mint Cordial

1 small bottle   **2½–3 hours**   **1 month, refrigerated**

Ingredients

50–100g (1¾–3½oz) peppermint, Moroccan mint, or spearmint (garden mint) leaves (see Tip)

300g (10oz) granulated sugar

a few drops of natural green food colouring (optional)

a few drops of natural peppermint extract (if using spearmint)

Special Equipment

large bowl

fine sieve

large saucepan

sterilized long-necked funnel

sterilized bottle

MAKE A PASTE

Put the mint leaves and sugar in a large bowl and crush them into a paste using the end of a rolling pin or the pestle from a pestle and mortar.

Tip This quantity of mint leaves gives a delicate flavour; if you prefer a more powerful punch, use double the amount of leaves.

Pour 300ml (10fl oz) of boiling water into the bowl and stir to combine. Cover the bowl and leave for at least 2 hours or until the water has cooled and the flavours have infused.

COOK THE CORDIAL

Set a sieve over a saucepan and strain the mixture into the pan. Press the leaves to extract the last of the juice. Cook the mix over a moderate heat, stirring until the sugar has dissolved. Then turn up the heat and boil for 2 minutes.

POUR INTO BOTTLES

Remove the pan from the heat, stir in the food colouring and peppermint extract, if using. Pour the syrup into a bottle using the funnel. Seal the bottles, leave to cool, and label. Store in the fridge.

Tip You can serve this cordial diluted with still or sparkling water, or mix it with vodka and ice for a refreshing cocktail.

Blackcurrant Cordial

1 large
bottle

20 minutes

6–8 weeks

Ingredients

450g (1lb) blackcurrants

225g (8oz) sugar

zest and juice of 1 lemon

Special Equipment

large saucepan

muslin

sterilized long-necked funnel

sterilized bottle

MAKE THE JUICE

Put the blackcurrants, sugar, and 250ml (8fl oz) water in a saucepan and cook over a gentle heat, stirring until the sugar has dissolved.

Simmer over a low heat for 5–8 minutes until the juices from the blackcurrants start to run.

Remember To extract the maximum amount of juice use the back of a wooden spoon or a potato masher to gently crush the fruit as it cooks.

POUR INTO A BOTTLE

Remove the pan from the heat, and stir in the lemon juice. Then strain the liquid through a funnel lined with muslin into a bottle.

Why? The muslin captures the blackcurrant skins, and ensures that the juice is beautifully clear.

Seal the bottle, leave to cool, label, and store in the fridge.

Tip For a thirst-quenching drink full of fizz, dilute 2 tablespoons of cordial with chilled sparkling water, and enjoy!

How to **Bottle Fruit in Syrup**

Bottling is a great way to prolong the harvest, providing sophisticated desserts at any time of year. The fruit is packed into jars, covered in syrup, and then boiled in the jar (heat processed) to remove both bacteria and air. This results in a strong vacuum seal that allows long storage times.

Tip You can add extra flavour to the syrup with whole spices such as cinnamon, cloves, a vanilla pod, or even fresh leaves like lavender, mint, or scented geranium. Add with the sugar and remove when the syrup is ready (see p.57 for how to make a spice bag).

Making sugar syrup

Sugar syrup keeps the flavour and texture of bottled fruit as intact as possible – and sometimes improves the flavour! Boil sugar and water in a pan over a gentle heat for 1–2 minutes, stirring to dissolve all the sugar so there are no grainy bits. For every 600ml (1 pint) water, use 115g (4oz) sugar for a light syrup, 175g (6oz) for medium, and 250g (10oz) for heavy.

Packing the fruit

Cut the fruit into halves or quarters and pack into warm, sterilized jars. Pour in the syrup up to the brim. For screw-top jars, fit a new seal, screw on the lid, then release it by a quarter turn. For clip jars, fit the rubber ring onto the lid and clamp the lid down. The rubber ring separates the top of the jar and the lid so air can escape when it's heated.

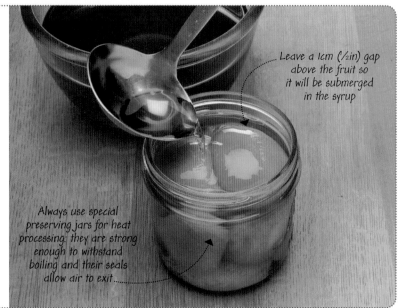

Leave a 1cm (½in) gap above the fruit so it will be submerged in the syrup

Always use special preserving jars for heat processing: they are strong enough to withstand boiling and their seals allow air to exit

Heat processing the jars

Place a folded tea towel or trivet in the base of a large stainless steel pan and put the jars on top; the jars will crack if placed directly on the base of the pan. Wrap the jars with tea towels to ensure they don't touch. Fill the pan with enough warm water to come 2.5cm (1in) above the jars. Cover the pan and bring slowly to a simmer, then heat for the required time (see table). Use tongs to remove the jars and immediately tighten the clips or screw-top lids. Test the seals 24 hours after heat processing. Try to prise off each lid with one fingernail. If it remains firmly in place, the seal is airtight and the jar is safe to store.

Water-bath Heat Processing Times

To ensure all the air is evacuated the jars and their contents must be heated through completely. Heat processing times therefore vary according to the contents of the jar. This table provides typical simmering times for popular fruits, assuming a starting temperature of the water of 38°C (100°F), and that it reaches a simmering point of 88°C (190°F) in 25–30 minutes. Use a sugar thermometer to gauge the correct temperatures.

Fruit	Heat processing time (minutes)
Apples (sliced)	2
Apricots (halved/sliced)	10
Blackberries (whole)	2
Blackcurrants (whole)	2
Blueberries (whole)	2
Boysenberries (whole)	2
Cherries (whole)	10
Citrus fruits (sections)	10
Cranberries (whole)	2
Figs (with lemon juice)	60–70
Gooseberries (whole)	10
Kumquats	10
Loganberries (whole)	2
Mulberries (whole)	2
Nectarines and peaches (halved/sliced)	20
Pears (halved/sliced)	40
Plums, all types (halved/sliced)	20
Quinces (sliced)	30
Raspberries (whole)	2
Red- and white currants (whole)	2
Rhubarb (stewed)	10
Strawberries (whole/sliced)	2
Tayberries (whole)	2

Peaches in Syrup

Peaches bottled in syrup make a glorious preserve that
can be enjoyed long after the peach season is over. Like
most fruits, peaches bottle well and require minimal
preparation before being heat processed to
preserve them for several months.

2 small jars   **15 minutes plus heat processing**   **12 months if heat processed**

Ingredients

115–250g (4–10oz) granulated sugar (see method)

4–5 just-ripe peaches

Equipment

saucepan

sharp knife

chopping board

screw-top or clip jars with lids and new rubber seals

ladle

stainless steel preserving pan

tea towels or trivet

tongs

granulated sugar   **peaches**

saucepan   **sharp knife**

chopping board   **screw-top jars**

ladle   **preserving pan**   **tea towels**   **tongs**

1 To make the syrup put the sugar in a pan, add 600ml (1 pint) of water, bring gently to the boil, and boil for 1–2 minutes.

Remember Choose a light, medium, or heavy syrup depending on how tart the fruit is, or how sweet you want it to taste (see p.116). It won't affect the longevity of the preserve, but it does dictate the amount of sugar you need to use.

Use the approriate amount of sugar for the "weight" of the syrup you intend to create

Handle the fruit as little as possible so it doesn't bruise

2 Skin the peaches, cut them in half, and carefully remove the stones. Reserve a few peach stones if you want to use the kernels to add a slightly bitter almond flavour.

Help! If the peach skins don't peel off easily, dip them in a bowl of boiling water for 30 seconds and try peeling the skins again.

3 Pack the peach halves into warm sterilized screw-top jars, leaving a gap of 1cm (½in) at the top. Crack the peach seeds with a nutcracker or clean pair of pliers to obtain the kernels, if using, and add with the peaches. Fill each jar with the hot syrup, ensuring the peaches are completely covered.

Tip Place the empty jars on a sheet of newspaper before filling to catch any syrup drips or spills.

Carefully pack the fruit as tightly as possible without bruising it, as it will shrink during heat processing

After sealing the lids, turn them back a quarter-turn to ensure air can escape

4 Tap the filled jars gently on the work surface and swivel them to remove any air bubbles. Fit the lids firmly – but remember to loosen them enough to allow air to evacuate during processing. Heat process the jars in a water bath (see p.117 for timings). Carefully remove the jars and tighten the lids immediately.

5 Leave the bottled fruits for 24 hours, then test each seal. If the seal is airtight (see p.117), refasten the lid and store the jar.

Tip If you use screw-top jars with metal lids, the slightly concave lid and lack of "give" once pressed indicates that you have a seal. You can test clip jars by releasing the catch and upturning them over a bowl: the vacuum should hold the lid – and its contents – in place.

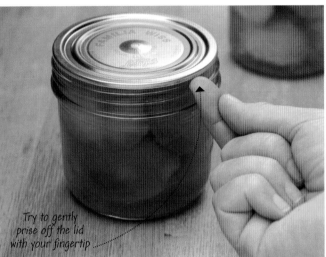

Try to gently prise off the lid with your fingertip

How to store

Label and store the heat-processed jars in a cool, dark place, where they will keep for up to 12 months. Once you have opened a jar, store it in the fridge and use it within 2 weeks.

Did anything go wrong?

The lid lifts easily when you test the seal. The heat processing was not successful; it has failed to evacuate all the air from the jar to create the necessary vacuum to preserve the fruit. The good news is that although it won't keep for long, you can still eat the contents. Store in the fridge and eat within 2 weeks.

Try other fruits

Good fruits to bottle include greengages, plums, pears, nectarines, raspberries, and blueberries.

Make sure the fruit you choose for bottling is firm, fresh, and without any discolouration, blemishes, or bruises.

Try more Bottled Fruit recipes ▶ ▶ ▶

Figs in Honey Syrup

2 small jars · **1 hour plus heat processing** · **12 months if heat processed**

Ingredients

250ml (8fl oz) clear honey

2 thinly pared strips of washed lemon zest (about 1cm/½in wide)

juice of 1 lemon (approx. 2 tbsp)

approx. 16 small ripe figs, or 12 large figs, washed and dried

PREPARE THE FIGS

Cook the honey, lemon zest and juice, and 500ml (16fl oz) of water in a saucepan over a gentle heat, stirring until the honey has dissolved. Bring the mix to the boil and boil for 3 minutes.

Carefully lower the figs into the boiling syrup and boil for another 2 minutes.

PACK THE JARS

Using a slotted spoon, transfer the figs from the pan to warm sterilized screw-top or rubber seal preserving jars.

Careful! Don't squash the figs too much as you fill the jars, or they may split and lose their shape.

Remove and discard the zest from the syrup. Pour the syrup into the jars to completely cover the figs. Tap each jar gently on the work surface to release any air bubbles in the syrup. Fit the metal lids or rubber bands and seal the jars. If you are using screw-top jars, loosen the lids by a quarter turn.

HEAT PROCESS THE JARS

Put a tea towel or trivet in the base of a preserving pan or large, heavy-based saucepan. Wrap the jars with tea towels to ensure they don't knock against each other during heat processing,

and place them in the pan. Fill the pan with enough warm water to cover the jars by 2.5cm (1in). Then cover the pan, and bring slowly to a simmer. Heat for the required time (see p.117).

SEAL, TEST, AND STORE

Remove the jars with tongs and tighten the lids if using screw-top jars.

Careful! Use a tea towel to protect your hands from the heat of the jars as you tighten the lids.

Leave the jars to cool for 24 hours before testing the seals. If the seal is airtight, you can refasten the lids and store the jars in a cool, dark place. Refrigerate after opening and use within 2 weeks.

Remember If heat processing has failed to create a strong vacuum seal, you can still enjoy the flavoured fruit and syrup: treat it as an opened jar and consume within 2 weeks.

Clementines in Caramel Syrup

1 large jar

25 minutes plus heat processing

12 months if heat processed

Ingredients

175g (6oz) granulated sugar

10 small clementines, peeled, white pith scraped off with a knife

MAKE THE SYRUP

Put the sugar and 100ml (3½fl oz) cold water in a saucepan and stir well. Heat gently without stirring until the sugar has dissolved.

Turn up the heat and boil rapidly for 5–8 minutes or until the syrup becomes a golden caramel colour. Pour in 200ml (7 fl oz) hot water. Stir until the caramel has dissolved and bring back to the boil.

Careful! The boiling caramel syrup will tend to spit as you stir it, so protect your hand with a tea towel or cloth.

PACK THE JARS

Place the fruits in a warm sterilized screw-top or rubber seal preserving jar, leaving 1cm (½in) of space at the top. Pour the syrup into the jar to cover the clementines completely. Tap the jar gently on a work surface to release any air bubbles in the syrup. Fit the metal lid or rubber band and seal the jar. If you have a screw-top jar, loosen the lid by a quarter turn.

HEAT PROCESS THE JARS

Put a tea towel or trivet in the base of a preserving pan or heavy-based saucepan. Wrap the jar in a tea towel for extra protection and place it in the pan. Fill the pan with enough warm water to cover the jar by 2.5cm (1in). Then cover the pan, and bring slowly to a simmer. Heat for the required time for citrus fruits (see p.117).

SEAL, TEST, AND STORE

Remove the jar with tongs and tighten the lid if using a screw-top jar.

Careful! Use a tea towel to protect your hands from the heat of the jar as you tighten the lid.

Leave the jar to cool for 24 hours and test the seal. If the seal is airtight, you can refasten the lid and store the jar in a cool, dark place. Refrigerate after opening and use within 2 weeks.

Remember If heat processing has failed to create a strong vacuum seal, you can still enjoy the fruit and caramel syrup: treat it as an opened jar and consume within 2 weeks.

How to **Dry Fruit and Vegetables**

Dehydration is one of the oldest-known methods of food preservation, probably because it is so simple and extremely effective: it draws out all the moisture that unwanted microorganisms, such as bacteria and mould, require to survive. The only thing you need in abundance is time, as it takes many hours to dry the produce properly.

Air-dry flat

Leave small items, such as little mushrooms, whole

The produce is ready when it has shrivelled to about half its original size, but is still pliable

PREPARE THE PRODUCE

Air-drying is a slow process, but placing the produce near a heat source speeds up the evaporation. Slice fresh fruit or vegetables thinly into small pieces. Arrange on baking trays or wire racks lined with kitchen paper. Ensure no pieces overlap or touch each other.

DRY OVER A SOURCE OF HEAT

Place the trays or racks 5–10cm (2–4in) above a heat source, such as on a wood-burning stove, radiator, or in a warm airing cupboard, and leave overnight. When the produce has dried, remove from the heat source, but leave on the tray until completely cold.

Air-dry hanging up

You can also dry orange and lemon peel by hanging up

Hang the herb bundles at regular intervals

Air can circulate easily around produce like herbs if they are hung up to air-dry. Tie the herbs into bundles with kitchen string and hang from a piece of thick string tied across an airy, dry room and away from direct sunlight. Leave the herbs for at least 2 weeks to dry thoroughly.

Oven-dry

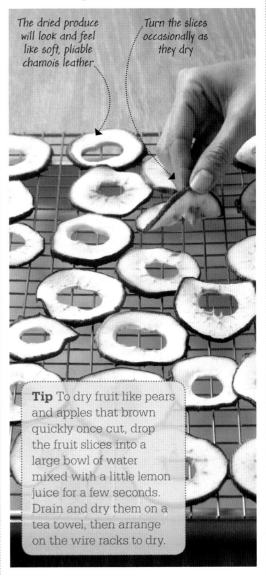

The dried produce will look and feel like soft, pliable chamois leather

Turn the slices occasionally as they dry

Tip To dry fruit like pears and apples that brown quickly once cut, drop the fruit slices into a large bowl of water mixed with a little lemon juice for a few seconds. Drain and dry them on a tea towel, then arrange on the wire racks to dry.

Slice fruit or vegetables into small pieces 5mm–1cm (¼–½in) thick. Arrange in a single layer on wire racks set over baking trays. Place in an oven set at its lowest temperature of 50–60°C (120–140°F/Gas ¼), for up to 24 hours. Leave the oven slightly ajar, using a skewer, to create an airflow.

Oven-dried Tomatoes

Drying tomatoes in the oven is an easy way of achieving
the same intense, rich flavour of sun-dried tomatoes, now
a commonplace ingredient in modern cooking. With
tomatoes so abundant in season, oven-drying makes
a great way of using up spare produce.

3 medium jars **10 minutes plus drying** **2 weeks (12 months if frozen)**

Ingredients

3kg (6½lb) ripe, firm,
    medium-sized tomatoes

2–3 tsp salt

olive oil to cover (optional)

Equipment

sharp knife

chopping board

wire racks

baking trays

sterilized jars with lids

tomatoes   **salt**

jars with lids   **olive oil**

wire racks   **chopping board**

sharp knife

baking trays

1 Check the tomatoes and remove any that are blemished or bruised. Use a sharp knife to cut round tomatoes in half horizontally and plum tomatoes vertically. Score a cross in each half with a sharp knife and push up the centre.

Why? Pushing up the centre of each scored tomato helps to expose more of the flesh to the drying air.

Push up the centre of the tomatoes with your fingertips

Just a pinch of salt will be enough to start drawing out moisture

2 Arrange the tomatoes with their crossed sides facing up on wire racks set over baking trays. Sprinkle each lightly with salt and leave for a few minutes. Then turn the halves over, taking care that the tomatoes are not touching each other.

Why? Sprinkling the tomatoes with salt helps to start drawing out moisture. The baking trays will catch all the juice.

3 Put the trays in the oven on a low setting, 60°–80°C (150°–175°F/Gas ¼–½), and dry for 8–12 hours, checking regularly to ensure they are not burning. When the tomatoes are dry, remove from the oven and leave to cool on the racks.

Tip Prop the oven door open very slightly by inserting a skewer between the frame and the door, to ensure the tomatoes dry out rather than cook.

Dried tomatoes should leave no residue when pressed in the centre

4 Pack the tomatoes into sterilized jars, either dry or completely covered in olive oil so they become softer. If storing in oil, tap the jars gently on the work surface to remove any air pockets.

Why? Tomatoes in oil are softer and less chewy than dry ones. This makes them more suitable for salads or as an antipasto, as they can be eaten straight from the fridge.

Cover the tomatoes completely with the oil

How to store

Keep the packed tomato jars in the fridge and use within 2 weeks.

To store the dried tomatoes for longer, freeze on open trays, pack them into small freezer bags, and freeze for up to 12 months. To use, allow the tomatoes to thaw, then pack them into a sterilized jar and pour in olive oil to cover completely, if preferred. Store in the fridge and use within one week.

Did anything go wrong?

If the tomatoes taste slightly toasted or look burnt around the edges, they may have become mouldy. Throw the produce away and, next time, make sure to keep the oven on its lowest setting and check the tomatoes regularly.

If the tomatoes have a slightly metallic taste to them, next time cover the wire racks with a cheesecloth before you arrange the tomato halves on them.

Try other vegetables

Try drying thinly sliced beetroots, carrots, and parsnips to make vegetable crisps.

Try drying more fruit and vegetables ▶ ▶ ▶

Dried Mushrooms

2 small jars | **15 minutes plus drying** | **9–12 months (12 months if frozen)**

Ingredients

450g (1lb) chestnut, shiitake, or buna-shimeji mushrooms, or freshly picked wild mushrooms

PREPARE THE MUSHROOMS

Thickly slice large mushrooms and leave small ones whole. Lay some kitchen paper over wire racks and arrange the mushrooms on top, making sure none of them overlap.

LEAVE TO DRY

Place the racks of mushrooms 5–10cm (2–4in) above a wood-burning stove, radiator, boiler, Aga, night storage heater, or warm airing cupboard and leave overnight. Alternatively, place the racks in the oven on its lowest setting – 50–60°C (120–140°F/Gas ¼) – for several hours.

Tip Prop the oven door open slightly with a skewer to ensure it doesn't get too hot and to keep the air circulating.

The mushrooms are dried when they have shrunk to half their size, but are still pliable. Store the dried mushrooms in glass jars in a cool, dark place. Alternatively, freeze on open trays, pack into freezer bags or pots, and store in the freezer.

Careful! Make sure the mushrooms are completely cold before you put them in glass jars. Any steam trapped inside will condense, creating a damp environment and thereby causing the mushrooms to deteriorate.

Tip Add a few grains of rice to each jar to help the mushrooms stay as dry as possible. The grains act as a desiccant, absorbing any trapped moisture.

Dried Apples

2 small jars

15–20 minutes plus drying

6 months (12 months if frozen)

Ingredients

2 tbsp lemon juice or ½ tsp citric or ascorbic acid (vitamin C powder)

1kg (2¼lb) ripe apples, washed, cored, and sliced into 3–5mm (⅛–¼in) thick rings

PREPARE THE APPLE RINGS

Pour 600ml (1 pint) of water into a bowl, add the lemon juice or citric or ascorbic acid, and stir. Drop a small batch of apple rings into the water, lift them out, drain on a tea towel, and arrange on wire racks, making sure they don't overlap.

Why? Dipping the apple slices in acidulated water prevents them from browning.

Place the racks in the oven on its lowest setting 50–60°C (120–140°F/Gas ¼) for 8–24 hours, depending on the temperature. Turn the slices occasionally as they dry.

Help! If the prospect of drying apple rings for such a long time seems daunting, you can dry them in stages over several days if you prefer.

STORE IN JARS

The apple rings are ready when they have shrunk, are pliable, and feel like soft chamois leather. Take them out of the oven, cover with kitchen paper, and leave for 12–24 hours. Turn often as they cool to evaporate as much moisture as possible.

Pack the dried rings into airtight jars and store in a cool, dark place. Make sure they are completely cold before you do this. If freezing, freeze the dried apples on open trays, then pack into freezer bags and store in the freezer.

Careful! Check the dried rings regularly for any signs of mould or deterioration and discard any that aren't in perfect condition.

Try other fruits

Stoned fruits For drying stoned fruits such as apricots, halve the fruits, remove the stones, and dry the halves cut-side up.

Thick-rind fruits For fruits with thick rind or peel such as melons and bananas, remove the rind or peel first and take out any seeds.

Thin-skin fruits Dip fruits with thin skins such as grapes into boiling water for 30 seconds to split the skins. Then drain and pat dry, and oven-dry.

Large fruits Larger fruits such as peaches and figs should be dried by cutting in half and drying cut-side up.

3

Take It Further

Now that you have mastered some of the
most valuable preserving skills, it's time
to become more adventurous. This chapter
covers a range of more unusual recipes that
broaden the horizons of the home-preserver.
Why rely on ready-made when you can
learn the art of curing, try your hand at
butter- and cheese-making, and even brew
your own alcohol?

In this section, learn to prepare or make:

How to **Make Marmalade**

Marmalade – a gelled fruit spread, like jam – is always made with citrus fruit, which gives it its unique tangy flavour. Preparing marmalade builds on your technical knowledge of jam-making by incorporating a straightforward stage of cooking the hard peel slowly for a time to soften it first before adding the sugar.

The citrus shells should feel softened if you test them with a wooden spoon

Tip Make sure the peel is soft enough before combining with the sugar, as sugar prevents any further softening.

Boiling shells, pith, and pips

To soften the peel, and to extract maximum pectin, which is concentrated in the peel, pith and pips, put the pips and any spare pith in a muslin bag (see p.57). Place the bag, along with the shells, in a pan of water, half-cover, and boil for 1 hour or until the shells are soft.

Cut the soft peel into short shreds ......

Cutting the peel

Allow the citrus shells to cool. Once they are cool enough to handle, use a sharp knife to cut the cooked citrus shells into evenly sliced strands on a chopping board. Chop the strands into thin, medium, or thick shreds depending on how you like your marmalade.

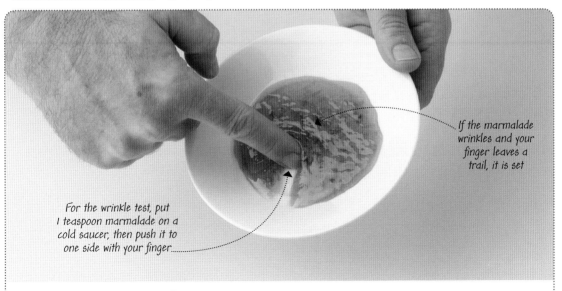

If the marmalade wrinkles and your finger leaves a trail, it is set

For the wrinkle test, put I teaspoon marmalade on a cold saucer, then push it to one side with your finger ......

Wrinkle test and flake test

Marmalades usually take 5–20 minutes boiling time to set, depending on how much pectin the batch contains. There are two set tests: a flake test and a wrinkle test. For the flake test, tilt 1 teaspoon marmalade. If the last of the mixture falls in a flat flake rather than a stream, it is set.

Orange Marmalade

Like jam, preparing this classic, bittersweet preserve is a systematic process. The citrus peel must be prepared before boiling the marmalade for a set. Marmalade is not just for breakfast; use it as a glaze for oven-baked ham (see p.183), as a topping, with desserts, or as a filling for cakes.

2 small jars   **1¾–2 hours**   **12 months**

Ingredients

1kg (2¼lb) large sweet oranges,
   scrubbed and stalks removed
   (or see variation below)

2 lemons, unwaxed

1kg (2¼lb) granulated sugar

Equipment

sharp knife

chopping board

muslin

string

preserving pan or large,
   heavy-based saucepan

large wooden spoon

sugar thermometer

wide-mouthed jam funnel

ladle

slotted spoon (optional)

jars with lids or with cellophane
   covers and elastic bands

discs of waxed paper

Seville Marmalade variation

Replace the large, sweet oranges with
small, bitter Seville oranges. They
have a thick, rough skin, tart flesh,
and lots of seeds, which makes them
high enough in pectin to give a
well-set marmalade. Use the same
quantity of Seville oranges, 1 lemon,
and 1.1kg (2½lb) of granulated sugar.

sweet oranges   **lemons**

granulated sugar

sharp knife

chopping board

string

muslin

wooden spoon   **sugar thermometer**

preserving pan

jam funnel   **ladle**

slotted spoon

jars

**discs of waxed
paper and
cellophane covers**

**elastic
bands**

1 Place one or two plates in the fridge or freezer to cool. Halve the oranges and lemons, squeeze their juice into a jug, and reserve it in the fridge so it stays fresh. Collect the pith and pips from the juicer, place them in a square of muslin, and tie into a bundle.

Tip Tie the muslin with a long string to make it easy to remove from the pan.

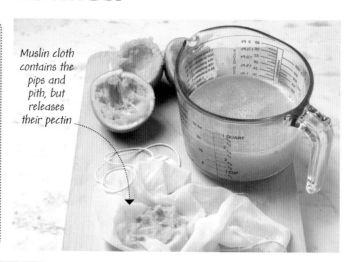

Muslin cloth contains the pips and pith, but releases their pectin

Reserve all the liquor from boiling the shells

2 Put the citrus shells in a preserving pan or large, heavy-based saucepan, add the muslin bag and 1.2 litres (2 pints) of water. Bring to the boil, then simmer for 1 hour or until soft. Tip the ingredients into a large colander set over a bowl. Scoop out the rest of the pith to leave the peel. Reserve the pith and liquid.

Tip Press the shells lightly to extract as much liquid as possible.

3 Cut the peel into short strands. Add some of the lemon peel for variety. Put the sliced peel, reserved liquid, and juice in the saucepan. Add the sugar and heat gently, stirring until it has dissolved. Boil rapidly for 5–20 minutes or until a set is achieved. Remove the pan from the heat while you test for a set (see p.135).

Remember Shorter boiling makes fresher marmalade, so test early.

Start testing for set early and retest every 2–3 minutes until you get a set

4 Once the marmalade has set, leave it for 10–12 minutes to cool and thicken slightly, so the strands will be evenly distributed. Skim off any scum, pot up into warm, sterilized jars, cover with waxed paper discs, and seal with lids, or with cellophane covers and elastic bands.

Careful! Don't let the marmalade cool too much – pot it up while still above 85°C (185°F).

Pot up before the marmalade cools too much to keep the sterilization process intact and to ensure the preserve won't spoil once potted

Use sterilized equipment (see p.11) to pot up the preserve

How to store

Label the jars and store them in a cool dark place for up to 12 months.

Did anything go wrong?

If the marmalade tastes peculiar or won't set, it may be that you have boiled it for too long; prolonged boiling affects both flavour and set.

If your peel is tough and hard, make sure you cook the citrus shells longer next time, as sugar hardens the peel. Alternatively, adding a lemon should help to overcome this problem.

Further tips

Although the basic method of making marmalade is the same, different recipes may require different quantities of sugar, depending on whether the fruit is bitter, tangy, or sweet.

Look for ripe citrus fruits with no blemishes or bruises for a superior-tasting marmalade. Don't choose fruits according to their colour. Many citrus fruits are fully ripe when their skins are still green.

Most non-organic oranges have a film of wax on their skin; scrub the skin well to remove this wax before cooking, or buy unwaxed citrus fruit.

Try other Marmalade recipes ▶ ▶ ▶

Clementine and Whisky Marmalade

3 medium jars	1¼ hours	9 months

Ingredients

900g (2lb) clementines, scrubbed and halved
with pips removed

juice of 2 large lemons

900g (2lb) granulated sugar

1–2 tbsp whisky (or brandy)

Put 1 or 2 small plates in the fridge to chill.

PREPARE THE CLEMENTINES

Blitz the clementines in a food processor using the pulse button until they are shredded but not mushy.

Tip If you don't have a food processor, squeeze the juice from the fruit and shred the skins finely with a sharp knife.

SOFTEN THE RIND

Put the chopped fruit in a preserving pan or a large, heavy saucepan and add 900ml (1½ pints) of water. Turn the heat up high, bring to the boil, then reduce to a simmer and cook over a gentle heat for 30 minutes or longer until the rind is soft.

BOIL TO A SET

Add the lemon juice and sugar to the pan. Keep the heat low and stir constantly until the sugar has dissolved and the sugar crystals are no longer visible. Turn the heat up high and bring to the boil. Keep the mixture in the pan at a rolling boil for 20–30 minutes, or until it thickens and reaches the setting point.

TEST FOR A SET

Take the pan off the heat and do a wrinkle test to see if the fruit mixture has set. Place a teaspoon of the mixture on a chilled plate, wait

for 60 seconds, and then push it with your finger. If it offers resistance and wrinkles as you push it, it has reached setting point. If the mixture hasn't set, bring it back to a rolling boil for another minute and test again.

POT UP THE MARMALADE

Once the marmalade has set, stir in the whisky (or brandy, if using) and leave the marmalade in the pan to cool for a few minutes.

Why? Allow the mixture to cool in the pan so that the fruit sinks from the surface and becomes more evenly distributed through the hot liquid.

Ladle the marmalade into sterilized jars. Cover with discs of waxed paper, seal, and label. Store in a cool, dark place. Once opened, keep refrigerated.

Pink Grapefruit Marmalade

4 large jars | **2–2½ hours plus time to steep** | **1 year**

Ingredients

3 Florida pink grapefruit, weighing approx. 750g (1lb 10oz), washed

2 lemons, washed

approx. 1.5kg (3lb 3oz) granulated sugar (see below)

Remember Before starting, weigh the grapefruit whole and double it to calculate the quantity of sugar required. As a general rule you will need double the weight of sugar to fruit.

Put 1 or 2 small plates in the fridge to chill.

PREPARE THE PEEL

Carefully peel the rind from the grapefruit and lemons and cut the rinds into very thin slivers.

Careful! Do not to leave any pith on the rinds, as it will make the marmalade bitter. Reserve any pith that you cut away, however, as you need to make use of its pectin content to achieve a good set.

Squeeze and reserve the juice from the lemons and grapefruit. After juicing, you are left with the thick pith "shells" of the grapefruit; reserve these.

Place any pips and pared off pieces of pith in a small bowl, add just enough cold water to cover, and set aside. Put the rind slivers, juice, and 1.3 litres (2¼ pints) of water in a bowl, cover, and leave to stand overnight. Chop the grapefruit shells, tie them up in a piece of muslin, and leave overnight.

SOFTEN THE RIND

Transfer the rind, juice, and water mixture to a preserving pan or large, heavy saucepan. Drain the water from the soaked pips and pith and also add to the pan. Transfer the pips and pith to the muslin bag of grapefruit shells and also add to the pan. Simmer for 1½–2 hours, stirring occasionally, or until the rind is very soft and the mixture has reduced by about half. Remove the muslin bag, allow to cool slightly, and squeeze out any juice back into the pan. Discard the bags.

BOIL TO A SET

Add the sugar and, on a low heat, keep stirring until it has dissolved. Then bring to the boil, and keep at a rolling boil for 20–30 minutes or until the mixture looks like it has thickened to setting point.

Take the pan off the heat. Do the wrinkle test to see if the mixture has set (see p.135). If the mixture hasn't set, bring it back to a rolling boil for a further minute and test again.

POT UP THE MARMALADE

When the marmalade has set, skim off any scum with a slotted spoon and leave in the pan for a few minutes, so the fruit can distribute itself more evenly through the hot liquid. Stir the mixture gently to disperse the last of the rind and ladle the marmalade into sterilized jars. Cover with discs of waxed paper, seal, and label. Store in a cool, dark place. Once opened, keep refrigerated.

How to **Make Fruit Curd**

Fruit curds are one of the few preserves to include dairy produce – usually butter, but sometimes double cream – and eggs. Some recipes suggest cooking the ingredients from start to finish in one pan, but this increases the risk of overheating, and can make the mixture split. For greater control, cook the mix gently in a bowl in a pan of simmering water to give a superior, velvety result.

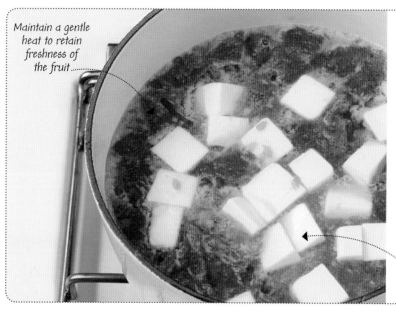

Maintain a gentle heat to retain freshness of the fruit

Melting and dissolving

Heat the fruit – use the juice, zest, and flesh of the citrus fruit if you want a robust curd, or just the juice if you prefer it smoother – with sugar and butter in a heavy-based saucepan. Keep stirring until the butter has melted, the sugar has dissolved, and no gritty bits remain.

Cut the softened butter into small chunks before adding, so it melts easily in the pan

This cooking method diffuses the heat

Adding the eggs

Transfer the mixture to a large heatproof bowl set in, or over, a pan of barely simmering water. This gentle method of cooking helps prevent the curd from splitting. Sieve the beaten eggs into the hot mixture through a fine-mesh sieve, stirring constantly to avoid scrambling them.

Stir constantly to distribute the heat and prevent any one part getting too hot and "cooking" the eggs

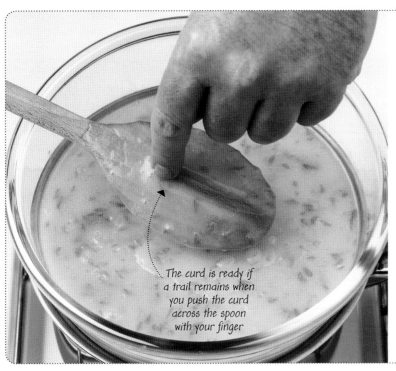

Achieving the correct consistency

Cook the mixture gently for 20–40 minutes, making sure the water does not get too hot and cause the curd to boil and split. Keep stirring constantly. The curd is ready when it is thick enough to coat the back of a wooden spoon.

The curd is ready if a trail remains when you push the curd across the spoon with your finger

Storing the curd

As soon as the curd is ready, remove it from the heat. Warm some sterilized jars and ladle the curd into them while it is still hot – the curd will thicken slightly as it cools. Seal immediately with waxed paper discs and cellophane seals, to store for later use. The curd can be stored for 1 month in the fridge.

Pot up the curd as soon as it is cooked

Use sterilized equipment to transfer the curd from the pan to warm jars

Lemon Curd

The great pleasure in making curds is that such
simple ingredients result in a gorgeously tangy, creamy
spread. Like fruit butters and cheeses, the main
ingredients of the lemon curd are fruit and sugar, but
butter and eggs provide richness.

3 small jars **15 minutes** **1 month refrigerated**

Ingredients

150g (5½oz) unsalted butter, diced

450g (1lb) caster sugar

juice and zest of 4 unwaxed lemons [juice about 350ml (12fl oz) in total]

4 small or medium eggs, lightly beaten

Equipment

sharp knife

chopping board

grater

large heatproof bowl

large saucepan

wooden spoon

fine mesh sieve

jars with lids or cellophane covers and elastic bands

waxed paper discs

butter

caster sugar

eggs

unwaxed lemons

sharp knife

chopping board

grater

heatproof bowl

saucepan

wooden spoon

fine mesh sieve

cellophane and waxed paper discs and elastic bands

jars

145

1 Prepare the zest by lightly grating the lemon rinds. Cut the lemons in half, squeeze out the juice, and reserve it. Put the lemon juice and zest in a pan and add the butter and sugar. Stir over a low heat until the butter melts and the sugar dissolves.

Careful! Only grate the yellow part of the rind: the white pith beneath has a bitter taste.

Use a fine grater for the lemon skins so the zest almost dissolves into the curd

The simmering water should come just a little way up the bowl

2 Transfer the mixture to a heatproof bowl and set it in a pan of gently simmering water.

Help! If you're worried that the mixture might curdle, slow down the cooking stage by resting the bowl over a smaller saucepan so that the base of the bowl doesn't touch the simmering water; the mixture will cook by the heat of the steam instead.

3 Strain the beaten eggs into the mixture using a fine mesh sieve and constantly stir the mixture as you do so.

Careful! Keep your eye on the mixture: don't leave it unattended or you could quickly end up with split curd. Stirring the mix not only helps to prevent the eggs scrambling, but it also ensures that the mixture doesn't overheat at the base, or stick to the bowl.

Sieve the beaten eggs to help prevent lumps forming and ensure a totally smooth finish

Stir the mixture constantly and ensure the heat remains low

The curd is set when it coats the back of a spoon and you can make a path with your finger.

4 Cook the curd in the bowl very gently for 20–40 minutes; keep the water simmering and top up if necessary – don't boil the pan dry.

Help! Curd that starts to bubble and boil is in danger of splitting. Remove the bowl from the heat, set it in a bowl of iced water, and stir with a spoon until it cools. Return it to a low heat and stir until it is the right consistency.

5 When the curd is ready, ladle it into warm sterilized jars while it is still hot, cover with waxed paper discs, and seal with the metal lids or cellophane covers.

Remember The finished curd will continue to thicken as it cools, but if you think that the curd isn't quite thick enough when you test it, return it to the heat and cook it for a little longer.

Curds have a relatively short shelf life once opened so pot into small jars

How to store

Store the jars of curd in the refrigerator for up to 1 month. Keep each jar refrigerated once opened.

Did anything go wrong?

The curd is bubbling furiously. Tip the mix into a large, cold bowl and whisk vigorously to reduce the heat and rescue the mixture before it curdles. See also step 4 above.

The curd separated. The mixture cooked too quickly; the heat may have been too high, or unevenly distributed through the liquid. Next time try suspending the bowl over the water, keep the heat very low, and keep stirring to ensure the mixture remains at an even temperature.

Try other fruits

Any fruit with a slight sharpness makes a good curd, such as apricots, blackcurrants, gooseberries, raspberries, limes, and grapefruit.

Try more Fruit Curd recipes ▶ ▶ ▶

Orange Curd

2 small jars

45–50 minutes

1 month refrigerated

Ingredients

juice and rind of 2 large oranges, scrubbed to remove the wax, and finely grated

juice of 1 lemon, freshly squeezed

175g (6oz) caster sugar

115g (4oz) unsalted butter, diced

4 large egg yolks, lightly beaten

COMBINE THE INGREDIENTS

Put the orange rind and juice in a saucepan with the lemon juice and mix well. Add the sugar and butter to the pan and heat gently until the butter has melted and the sugar has dissolved. Transfer this mixture to a heatproof bowl and allow to cool slightly.

COOK THE CURD

Sit the heatproof bowl in a pan of very gently simmering water; the water should come only a short way up the side of the bowl.

Remember If preferred, you can cook over a lower heat by resting the bowl over a smaller pan so that there is no contact between the water and the base of the bowl. The cooking time will be longer.

Sieve the egg yolks and stir in. Cook the curd very gently, stirring constantly, for about 25–30 minutes or until the mixture has thickened and coats the back of a spoon. Test for a set with your finger: if you can draw a path through the curd on the back of the spoon, the curd is ready to pot.

Careful! Be patient as the curd cooks. Stir constantly to ensure that heat is evenly distributed and do not allow it to boil because it will cause the mixture to separate.

POT THE CURD

Remove the cooked curd from the heat and ladle it into warm sterilized jars. Cover with discs of waxed paper, seal, and label. Keep refrigerated and use within 1 month of making.

Serve orange curd as a tangy accompaniment to ice cream, or use it as a filling for cakes.

Remember Curds do not have a very long shelf life and must be stored in the fridge.

Raspberry Curd

2 small jars   **45–50 minutes**   **1 month refrigerated**

Ingredients

250g (9oz) fresh raspberries

2 tbsp lemon juice, freshly squeezed

115g (4oz) unsalted butter, diced

150g (5½oz) caster sugar

4 large egg yolks and 1 large egg, lightly beaten

COMBINE THE INGREDIENTS

Process the raspberries in a food processor with the lemon juice, then sieve the pulp to remove any pips. Add the raspberry purée to a saucepan with the butter and sugar and heat gently until the butter has melted and the sugar has dissolved. Transfer this mixture to a heatproof bowl and allow to cool slightly.

Tip To speed up the cooking, gently warm the caster sugar in a low preheated oven for about 5 minutes before adding it to the purée.

COOK THE CURD

Place the heatproof bowl in a saucepan of very gently simmering water; the water should come only a short way up the side of the bowl.

Tip If preferred, you can cook over a lower heat by resting the bowl over a smaller pan so that there is no contact between the water and the base of the bowl. The cooking time will be longer.

Sieve the egg yolks and the egg into the bowl and cook over a very gentle heat, stirring constantly, for about 25–30 minutes or until the mixture has thickened and coats the back of a spoon. If you can leave a trail with your finger, the curd is ready.

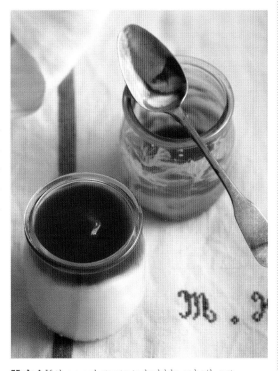

Help! If the curd starts to bubble or boil, act immediately to prevent it from curdling. Take the bowl off the heat. Either set it in a bowl of iced water and stir with a wooden spoon until the mixture cools, or tip the curd into a large cold bowl and whisk vigorously to reduce the temperature and distribute the heat more evenly.

POT THE CURD

Remove the cooked curd from the heat and ladle into warm sterilized jars. Cover with discs of waxed paper, seal, and label. Keep refrigerated and use within 1 month.

Serve raspberry curd as a topping for yogurt or with whipped cream and meringues for an indulgent treat.

How to **Make Butter**

Traditionally butter – and indeed cheese – were methods of preserving surplus milk. Although storing milk is no longer such a problem, making your own butter can be a fun and satisfying experience. It's also surprisingly quick. You don't need special equipment – just an electric whisk or food processor, and about 30 minutes of your time.

The mixture should look like yellow scrambled eggs as you near the end of whisking

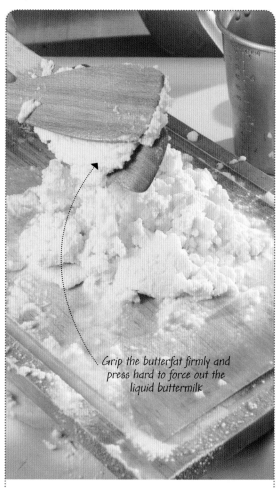

Grip the butterfat firmly and press hard to force out the liquid buttermilk

Make the butterfat

Butter is made from the fattiest parts of milk – or as we know it, cream. The first stage is to transform the cream into butterfat. Leave it to stand for a couple of hours to sour. Then whisk for a few minutes to recreate the churning used in traditional butter-making.

Extract the buttermilk

Whisking separates the cream into solid butterfat and a liquid called buttermilk. All the buttermilk must be thoroughly squeezed out as it otherwise quickly turns sour and spoils the butter. Grooved butter pats are traditionally used but spatulas work well.

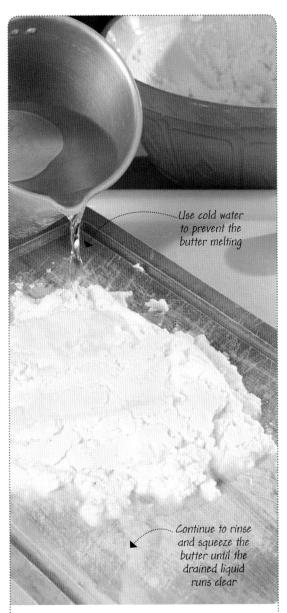

Use cold water to prevent the butter melting

Continue to rinse and squeeze the butter until the drained liquid runs clear

Push the butter down hard, or roll it tightly to expel air bubbles that can cause it to spoil

Wash the butter

As you squeeze out the buttermilk you can reserve it for soda bread and cake recipes or simply for drinking. Rinse the butterfat with cold water after each squeeze; when the water runs clear all the buttermilk will have been expelled and the fat is ready to mould.

Pack and shape the butter

Pack the butter firmly into a butter mould, adding salt between each layer to extend its shelf life. Alternatively spread the butter in a thin layer and sprinkle it with salt. Mix together thoroughly, then shape the salted butter into a rectangular slab or a roll.

Salted and Unsalted Butter

Butter is quick and simple to make – and if you happen to
have some spare cream in the fridge, it's a clever way to
use it up. Add fresh herbs, crushed peppercorns, or minced
garlic cloves to the finished butter and use it with fried fish
or steak or to add flavour to sauces.

| 500g (1lb 2oz) | Approx. 25 minutes | Up to 3 weeks if salted |

Ingredients

1.2 litres (2 pints) double cream, left at room temperature for 3 hours

1 tsp fine salt (optional)

Equipment

electric hand whisk or food processor

large bowl

sieve

wooden chopping board

wooden spatulas or butter pats

butter mould, ramekins, or greaseproof paper

double cream　　　　**salt**

electric hand whisk

large bowl

sieve

wooden chopping board　　**butter mould**　　**wooden spatulas**

153

1 Pour the cream into a large, clean sterilized bowl. Whisk the cream for a few minutes with an electric hand whisk until it is of a whipped consistency with soft peaks.

Tip If preferred you can use a food processor to whisk the cream until it separates.

2 Keep whisking until the cream yellows, and resembles scrambled eggs. Whisk for a further 2–3 minutes, or until it has split into buttermilk liquid and fat solids. Drain off the buttermilk.

Careful! When the mixture splits it will be difficult to continue whisking without the buttermilk spraying out of the bowl. The low speed setting gives you time to react – and stop – quickly.

Use a low speed setting for the last minute of whisking

The mixture will look like a mass of small globules of fat

3 Place the solid butterfat in a sieve and wash it under cold water, before transferring it to a wooden board. Using wooden spatulas or butter pats, pick up clumps of butterfat and squeeze out the buttermilk.

Tip Soak your wooden utensils in iced water for about 30 seconds before you use them so they don't stick to the butter.

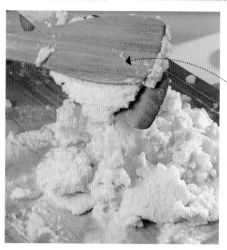

Avoid working the butterfat directly with your hands to prevent it from melting; use wooden utensils instead, which don't conduct heat

4 Continue squeezing the butterfat to expel buttermilk. Rinse the butter with cold water, then squeeze out more buttermilk, and repeat. The butter is ready when the water runs clear.

Why? The process of extracting all the buttermilk and washing the butterfat helps to extend the butter's shelf life, as buttermilk turns butter rancid.

Cold water helps to keep the butter cool while you work

5 Spoon or press the butterfat firmly into the butter mould or ramekins, or alternatively shape by hand into a roll or rectangle and wrap tightly in greaseproof paper. Store in the fridge and use within 7 days. If salting the butter, add the fat in layers and scatter salt over each layer.

Careful! Pack the butter in tightly to drive out air bubbles, which can spoil the butter.

How to store

Adding salt preserves the butter for 2–3 weeks in the fridge; alternatively freeze it for 2–3 months.

Did anything go wrong?

The cream doesn't seem to whip properly. You may be using homogenized cream. The homogenized cream will whip, but possibly not as well as you expect.

Try making flavoured butters

Add herbs and spices to the butter along with the salt to create your own flavoured butters. Try wholegrain mustard with dried thyme and sage; finely chopped chives, dill, or mint; finely chopped parsley and lemon zest; or minced garlic. Store in the fridge for about 1 week, or roll into convenient portions and freeze for up to 3 months.

Try making Soft Cheese ▶ ▶ ▶

How to **Make Soft Cheese**

Historically, making soft cheese was regarded as another way to use up spare milk, and its alternative name – cottage cheese – reveals its humble origins. No special equipment or sophisticated processes are needed: just curdle some milk and strain off the watery by-product to make mild-tasting curds that can be enhanced with additional flavours.

Use a slotted spoon to skim off the curds

Do not allow the milk to boil: remove it from the heat as soon as it starts to simmer

Strain the curds overnight in a muslin bag

Curdle the milk

Left to stand in a warm place, milk becomes more acidic, causing it to sour (or "curdle") and separate into curds and a watery whey. You can accelerate the process by gently warming milk in a saucepan then stirring in some lemon juice, which is naturally acidic.

Hang the curds

The soft cheese is made using the curds. Remove the curds from the liquid whey and allow them to dry out further by straining them overnight. The result is a soft cheese with a very mild taste, that is ready to flavour with herbs and spices.

Soft Cheese with Garlic and Herbs

Approx. 200g (7oz)   **1½–2 days**   **Up to 2 days**

Ingredients

1.2 litres (2 pints) whole milk

2 tbsp fresh lemon juice

½–1 clove garlic, finely chopped

2 tbsp freshly chopped mixed herbs,
    such as chives and parsley

sea salt and freshly ground black pepper

Special Equipment

muslin

string

MAKE THE CHEESE
Pour the milk into a large, heavy-bottomed saucepan and heat gently until it is just below the boil. As soon as the milk begins to simmer, remove the pan from the heat.

Stir in the lemon juice to encourage curds to form, then leave undisturbed for 10 minutes to curdle.

Remember The lemon juice increases the acidity of the milk, and speeds up the curdling process.

DRAIN THE CHEESE
Line a sieve with muslin and transfer the curds with a slotted spoon. Leave to strain for at least 30 minutes until most of the whey has drained off. Discard the whey.

Why? It is important to drain off all the liquid otherwise the cheese will be too soft and will not keep as long.

Pull the muslin up around the curds and squeeze to remove excess liquid. Tie the ends of the muslin with string and leave to strain overnight over a bowl in the refrigerator.

Tip Place the muslin in a sieve over a large mixing bowl to catch the remaining drips of whey; alternatively push a wooden spoon through the loops of the bag and suspend it over the bowl.

ADD THE FLAVOURINGS
Unwrap the soft cheese from the muslin and spread it out on a clean worktop or chopping board. Discard any whey that accumulated overnight.

Gently knead in the garlic, chives, and the rest of the seasoning until it is thoroughly mixed. Spoon the cheese into a clean pot, ramekins, or dishes and store in the fridge. Use within 2 days.

Tip The cheese will lose its texture and break down slightly after 2 days, but it's worth waiting for 24 hours before trying the cheese, to allow the flavours to mingle.

How to **Make Alcoholic Drinks**

Enjoying your own wine or cider need not be a distant dream. With some basic brewing equipment, careful preparation, and a little bit of patience you can make alcoholic drinks with delicious flavours from fruits, vegetables, and even flowers – simply add sugar and specialist wine or brewer's yeast and leave to ferment.

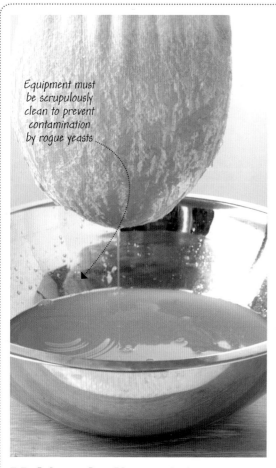

Equipment must be scrupulously clean to prevent contamination by rogue yeasts

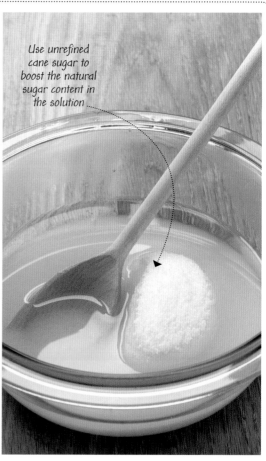

Use unrefined cane sugar to boost the natural sugar content in the solution

Making the liquor juice

Wine and brewer's yeasts contain specially selected microbes that break down or "feed on" very sugary acidic liquor and convert it to alcohol. It is usually necessary to add extra sugar to fruit juices to supplement their natural sugar content. Mash the fruit according to the recipe and strain the pulp with the help of a sterilized jelly bag, muslin cloth, or muslin-lined sieve set over a sterilized bowl. If you are making cider, add the sugar directly to the strained juice. If you are making wine, dissolve the sugar in a bowl of hot water and allow the mixture to cool before adding it to the prepared fruit.

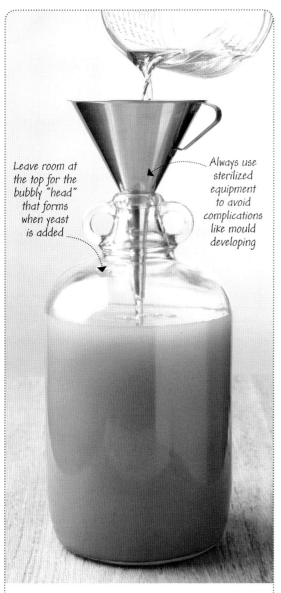

Leave room at the top for the bubbly "head" that forms when yeast is added

Always use sterilized equipment to avoid complications like mould developing

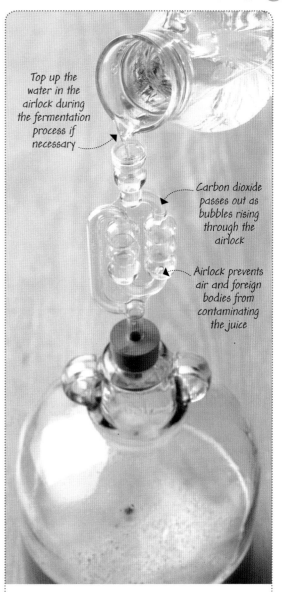

Top up the water in the airlock during the fermentation process if necessary

Carbon dioxide passes out as bubbles rising through the airlock

Airlock prevents air and foreign bodies from contaminating the juice

Ferment the liquor

Pour the juice through a sterilized funnel into a sterilized demijohn, leaving a reasonable head space at the top. Add the yeast. Specialist yeasts ensure consistent, predictable results and eliminate unwanted wild yeasts, such as those that naturally occur on grape skins.

Fit an airlock

Once fermentation is underway, fit an airlock to the demijohn and pour a little water into it to allow carbon dioxide to escape as bubbles while the juice ferments. The bubbles cease once fermentation is complete; the yeast eventually dies off and collects as clumps of sediment at the base of the demijohn.

Cider

Cider is made from fermented apple juice. You can use any
type of apple, including windfalls. Generally, the sharper
the variety, the drier the cider. Choose a dessert variety
if you prefer a sweet cider, or use one-third each of
bitter-sweet, sweet, and sharp apples for a delicious mix.

4 litres (7 pints)   **3 months**   **6 months**

apples

champagne yeast

cane sugar

Ingredients

3.5kg (7–8lb) apples, or
    4 litres (7 pints) apple juice

5g (⅛oz) champagne yeast

100g (3½oz) unrefined cane sugar

jelly bag

Equipment

food processor or electric fruit juicer

jelly bag or muslin-lined sieve

large bowl

hydrometer (to measure the specific
    gravity of liquids)

measuring jug

demijohn and siphon

long-spouted funnel

cotton wool

airlock and rubber bung

glass bottles

corks and a corker

food processor

bowl

hydrometer

demijohn
and
siphon

corks

measuring jug

long-
spouted
funnel

cotton wool   airlock   bottles

1 Check that the apples are in good condition and cut away any bruised parts. Place the apples in the freezer and leave them overnight. Allow the apples to thaw thoroughly, then process them in a food processor.

Why? Freezing the apples softens them by breaking down their fibrous walls.

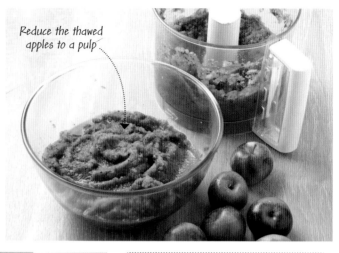

Reduce the thawed apples to a pulp

Strain the pulp in small batches if necessary

2 Strain the pulp through a jelly bag or clean, muslin-lined sieve set over a bowl until you have collected 4 litres (7 pints) of juice. Use a hydrometer to measure the gravity of the juice. It should read between 1,035 and 1,050.

Help! If the gravity is not within range, gradually dilute the juice with water until it is.

3 Add the sugar to the juice and keep stirring until it is dissolved. Using a sterilized funnel, pour the juice into a sterilized demijohn.

Remember Be scrupulous about sterilizing all your brewing equipment to eliminate unwanted contaminants. This prevents airborne microorganisms from contaminating the brew and causing it to deteriorate.

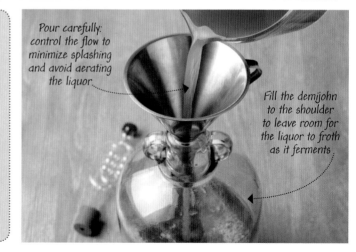

Pour carefully: control the flow to minimize splashing and avoid aerating the liquor

Fill the demijohn to the shoulder to leave room for the liquor to froth as it ferments

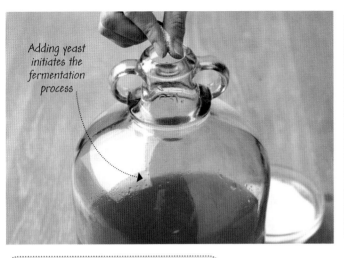

Adding yeast initiates the fermentation process

4 Add the yeast and seal the demijohn with cotton wool. Leave at room temperature for 2 days. When the frothing reduces, replace the cotton wool with a sterilized airlock and pour water into it. Leave for at least 2 weeks or until the airlock stops bubbling.

Why? Cotton wool allows carbon dioxide to escape more easily in the vigorous stage of fermentation, and excludes microorganisms.

5 Siphon the cider into bottles. The bottle must be below the level of the liquid in the demijohn. Put one end of the siphon in the demijohn, suck it like a straw to fill it with cider and swiftly insert the tube into the bottle. Lift each bottle as it fills to control the flow and move the tube to the next bottle.

Careful! Make sure fermentation is complete before you bottle the cider, or the bottles may explode.

Allow 2cm (³⁄₄in) of head space in case of expansion

How to seal and store

To seal, put a cork in the corker, place over the bottle, and pull the lever to insert the cork fully.

Leave cider for about 3 months in a dark place at room temperature (sunlight can cause it to spoil).

Store corked bottles sideways so the corks keep moist – dry corks shrink and let in too much air, which spoils the cider. Cider is best consumed within 6 months.

Did anything go wrong?

If your cider doesn't taste right, you may have put the demijohn in too warm or too cold a place during fermentation or you may not have sterilized your equipment properly. Alternatively, you may have stored the corked bottles upright and allowed the air in, spoiling the brew.

Your cider may also not taste right if you used baker's yeast instead of a speciality yeast. Always check the recipe and use the correct ingredients.

Try more Alcoholic Drink recipes ▶ ▶ ▶

Greengage Wine

4.5 litres
(1 gallon)

8 months

2 years

Ingredients

2kg (4½lb) greengages, washed

juice of 1 lemon

1 tsp pectolase (a pectolytic enzyme)

1 tsp wine yeast

1.5kg (3lb 3oz) unrefined cane sugar

Special Equipment

fermenting bin or large bucket

potato masher

muslin

PREPARE THE FRUIT

Put the greengages in the freezer overnight. This starts to break down the pectin that can otherwise turn the wine cloudy. Defrost thoroughly.

Stone the fruit, tip it into the fermenting bin, and mash it with a potato masher. Add the lemon juice and pour in 3.5 litres (6 pints) of boiling water. Allow to cool. Add the pectolase, which removes the remaining pectin from the juice. Cover and leave for 24 hours at room temperature.

Careful! Room temperature ranges from 15–25°C (59–77°F); if your room is hotter or colder than this, it will affect the result, so try to improve the conditions or find a different place to make the wine.

ADD THE YEAST

Add the yeast to the fruit mixture, cover and leave for 4–5 days in the dark at room temperature.

Tip the fruit mixture into a muslin cloth (fit the muslin inside a sterilized sieve if required) set over a sterilized bowl and collect the juice

ADD THE SUGAR

Put the sugar into a large jug. Pour in enough hot water to cover the sugar and stir until it has dissolved – add more hot water if you need to, and continue stirring until the sugar crystals are no longer visible. Cool, then stir the liquid into the juice.

Tip If you are using very ripe fruit, the wine may be a little sweet if you use the recommended quantity of sugar. For a drier wine, use a little less sugar.

LEAVE TO FERMENT

Using a sterilized funnel transfer the sugary juice into a sterilized demijohn then fit a sterilized airlock. Pour a little water into the airlock and then leave the liquid to ferment for 2 months at room temperature.

BOTTLE THE WINE

Check the airlock regularly. When there are no bubbles in the airlock, transfer the wine into sterilized bottles using a sterilized siphon. Leave 2cm (¾in) of space at the top of each bottle. Seal, label, and store in a cool, dark place for 6 months before opening.

Why? Leave space at the top in case temperatures fluctuate and the wine expands. The small amount of air at the top of the bottle also allows the wine to age without becoming oxidized.

Elderflower Champagne

4.5 litres (1 gallon)   **2 weeks**   **3 months**

Ingredients

1.25kg (2¾lb) unrefined cane sugar

8 large elderflower heads

2 lemons, sliced

juice of 2 lemons

4 tbsp white wine vinegar

Special Equipment

2 fermenting bins or large buckets

muslin

DISSOLVE THE SUGAR

Pour the sugar into a fermenting bin and add 8 litres (1¾ gallons) of boiling water. Cover, and allow to cool.

PREPARE THE FLOWERS

Gently shake the flower heads to remove any insects. Add the flower heads to the sugar solution.

Why? The elderflowers not only flavour the drink but the wild yeasts that are naturally present in the flowers are used for fermentation. No additional yeast is added so the champagne is only mildly alcoholic – if at all.

Add the lemon juice, lemon slices, and vinegar, cover with a clean cloth and leave for 24 hours.

STRAIN THE LIQUID

Pour the liquid through a fine sieve or muslin cloth into a sterilized bucket.

Tip Squeeze the flower heads as you strain the liquid to release the maximum amount of flavour.

BOTTLE THE WINE

Transfer the liquid into sterilized bottles using a sterilized long-necked funnel, leaving 2cm (¾in) of space at the top of each bottle. Seal, label, and store the bottles in a cool, dark place for 10–14 days.

Remember Closely monitor wine stored in plastic bottles. Keep the bottles in a dark place to prevent the plastic degrading. Check the bottles every day and release a little gas to prevent them swelling.

How to **Dry- and Wet-cure Fish**

Dry-curing white and oily fish with fine sea salt not only prolongs its shelf life by a few days, but also helps to develop its flavour and firm its texture, making it taste as good as cooked. Wet-curing fish by pickling it in vinegar and brine also adds richness and flavour. The vinegar acts in a similar way to heat, changing the structure of the fish's protein and effectively "cooking" it.

Dry-curing the fish

If you are arranging small fish in layers, sprinkle salt over each layer.

COVERING THE FISH IN A "CURE"
Put the fish in a shallow dish and sprinkle over a layer of fine sea salt to draw out moisture, which inhibits the growth of microbes. Cover with cling film and leave to cure in the fridge as stated in the recipe. Place a weight on top to remove more liquid and speed up the process.

Dry the fish carefully using kitchen paper.

DRYING THE FISH
Turn the fish every 12 hours. Moisture collects in the dish as the fillets cure; drain the liquid to prevent the fish reabsorbing it. Cured fillets should be firm in texture and easy to slice. Pat dry with kitchen paper to remove any excess salt and store for up to 2 days in the fridge.

Wet-curing the fish

Allow the fish to absorb the brine for 2–3 hours

SOFTENING THE FISH WITH BRINE
Soak the fish fillets in brine for a few hours, then drain and dry with kitchen paper. The brine penetrates the fish, inhibiting the growth of bacteria and drawing out moisture.

Leave the spices to steep in the vinegar

Keep the fish submerged in the vinegar

You can add additional flavourings

MAKING PICKLING VINEGAR
Slowly bring the vinegar, sugar, and spices to the boil in a stainless-steel pan. Simmer for 2 minutes, and allow to cool. A plain vinegar can also be used, but pickling vinegar adds flavour.

PICKLING IN THE VINEGAR
Place the fish in a sterilized jar and cover with vinegar. The longer the fish is pickled, the more mature its flavour. As vinegar is a preservative the fish keeps for longer than dry-cured fillets.

Practise DRY-CURING FISH

Gravadlax

Fresh fish is a delicate food, so it requires gentle
preserving methods to improve its flavour and taste.
This traditional Scandinavian method of salting salmon
to gradually alter its natural qualities is easy to try
using ordinary kitchen equipment.

1kg (2¼lb)   **2 days**   **3–4 days (fridge); 2 months (frozen)**

Ingredients

85g (3oz) caster sugar or soft light brown sugar (optional; see step 1)

30g (1oz) dill, chopped

1 tbsp lemon juice

75g (2½oz) fine sea salt

1 tsp freshly ground black pepper

2 x 500g (1lb 2oz) thick salmon fillets

Equipment

small bowl

clean tray, large enough to accommodate the salmon fillets

cling film

ladle or large spoon

kitchen paper

sharp knife

chopping board

caster sugar

dill

lemon juice

sea salt

black pepper

salmon

chopping board

cling film

small bowl

kitchen paper

sharp knife

ladle

1 Get your fishmonger to prepare two matching fillets of salmon, one from either side of the same fish, removing all the bones in the process. Make the dry-cure mix: put the sugar, dill, lemon juice, salt, and pepper in a small bowl and combine thoroughly.

Tip Use soft light brown sugar instead of caster sugar if you want a slightly deeper, richer flavour, and darker colour.

Spread the curing mix with your fingers and rub it into the flesh

2 Lay one of the salmon fillets, skin-side down, in the tray. Spread the curing mix evenly over the flesh.

Careful! Check for any stray bones by running your finger along the fillets before you add the cure.

3 Place the second salmon fillet on top of the first, flesh-side down. Wrap the fillets tightly in cling film, leaving the head and tail ends open so liquid runs out. Place a weight on top and leave to cure in the fridge for 48 hours.

Tip Compressing the fillets helps to squeeze moisture out. Place a plate or board on top of the fish and weigh it down with cans.

Lay one fillet carefully over the other to cover the curing mix completely

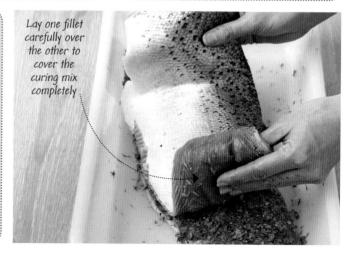

4 Turn the wrapped fish every 12 hours to compress each fillet thoroughly, and drain off the moisture drawn out of the fillets. After 48 hours remove the cling film, pat dry with kitchen paper, and slice with a sharp knife.

Remember The cured fish will be a bit smaller and much firmer than the original fillets.

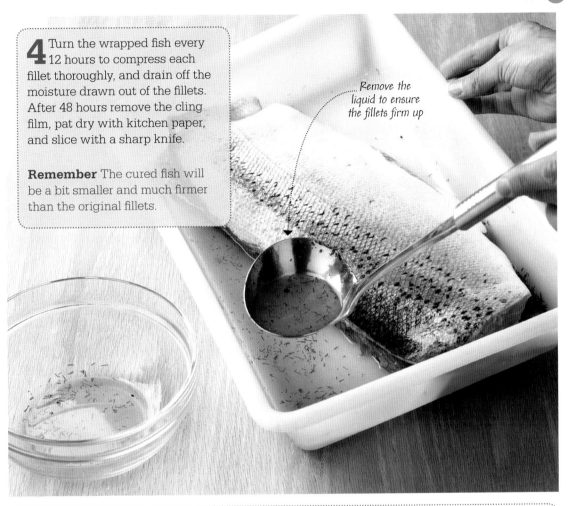

Remove the liquid to ensure the fillets firm up

How to store

Refrigerate the sliced gravadlax and eat it within 3–4 days. Alternatively, you can freeze it for up to 2 months.

Did anything go wrong?

The fish isn't firm enough to slice. It may still contain too much moisture. Continue curing for up to 5 days; use a heavier weight. Do not eat fish if you think it has spoiled, or fish that smells rancid.

Try other fish

Other fish to dry-cure include very fresh trout, mackerel, and halibut. Always use the freshest fish you can find.

If you use wild salmon, freeze it for at least 24 hours and leave to thaw in the fridge before dry-curing. Freezing kills the parasites that may be found in wild fish.

Try more Cured Fish recipes ▶ ▶ ▶

Rollmops

1 medium jar   3–4 days   1 month, refrigerated

Ingredients

6–8 very fresh herring fillets, descaled and trimmed, with any visible bones removed

1 red onion, finely sliced

6–8 pickled gherkins

For the brine

60g (2oz) sea salt per 450ml (15fl oz) of cold water

For the spiced vinegar

450ml (15fl oz) cider or white wine vinegar

1 tbsp light brown soft sugar

6 black peppercorns

6 allspice berries

1 blade of mace

3 bay leaves

1 dried chilli

Special Equipment

cocktail sticks

SOAK IN BRINE

Arrange the herring fillets in a large, shallow glass dish and pour the brine over the top to cover them completely. Leave to soak for 2–3 hours. Drain the brine and dry each fillet with kitchen paper.

Help! The amount of brine required depends on the number and size of the fillets as well as the size of the dish. To work out approximate quantities, fill the dish with water to about the half-way point and pour into a measuring jug. You can then calculate how much salt to dissolve in the water.

MAKE THE SPICED VINEGAR

Put all the ingredients for the spiced vinegar in a stainless steel saucepan and bring slowly to the boil. Simmer for 1–2 minutes, then set aside to cool.

ROLL THE FILLETS

Lay out the fillets skin-side down on a clean chopping board. Place an onion slice and a gherkin on the tail-end of a fillet and roll it up. Secure with a cocktail stick. Repeat with the rest of the fillets.

PACK THE JAR

Put the rollmops in a sterilized jar and pour over the cold spiced vinegar – including the spices – so that it covers the fish completely. Top up with extra vinegar, if needed. Seal and store in the fridge for 3–4 days to mature.

Remember Always keep the fish submerged in the vinegar to ensure they don't spoil.

Quick Salted Herrings

1 small jar   1–3 days if   1–2 weeks
             marinating

Ingredients

2 very fresh herring fillets, boned, with head,
   excess skin, and fins removed

small slivers of lemon peel (optional)

olive oil, to cover (if marinating)

For the cure mix

2 tsp fine sea salt

2 tsp caster sugar

1 tsp brandy

freshly ground black pepper

2 tsp fresh dill, chopped

CURE THE FILLETS

In a small bowl, combine the ingredients for
the cure mix.

Place the largest fillet skin-side down on a
clean plate. Spread the cure over the fillet, making
sure that the flesh is completely covered. Place the
second fillet on top of the first, skin-side up.

Wrap the fillet sandwich in cling film, weigh it
down with a heavy weight, and leave for 24 hours
in the fridge to cure. Leave the head and tail ends
of the cling film open so that liquid can run out of
the package when you turn the fillets.

Why? Wrapping the fillets in cling film holds
the sandwich together and ensures that the cure
remains in contact with the flesh throughout the
process, drawing out moisture and adding flavour.

Turn the fillets after 12 hours and drain off any
liquid. After 24 hours, the fillets should be firm and
ready to eat. Remove the cling film, drain, and pat
dry with kitchen paper.

The fillets can be refrigerated for up to 1 week:
transfer them to a clean plate, cover with cling film
and store in the fridge. For a deeper flavour (and
slightly longer shelf life of up to 2 weeks) try
marinating the fillets in oil.

MARINATE THE FILLETS

Slice the fillets thinly and remove the skins.
Place the fillets in a sterilized jar, add the lemon
peel (if required), and pour in enough oil to cover
the slivers of fillet completely. Leave in the fridge
for 48 hours to mature before eating

How to **Wet- and Dry-cure Meat**

Curing meat is an age-old preserving technique. Originally a cold cellar was required to achieve the right results, but these days a fridge makes the process more convenient. It's worthwhile preserving meat yourself: there's nothing like the taste of home-cured food, and it is an excellent way to flavour and extend the shelf life of cheaper cuts of meat.

Wet-cure method

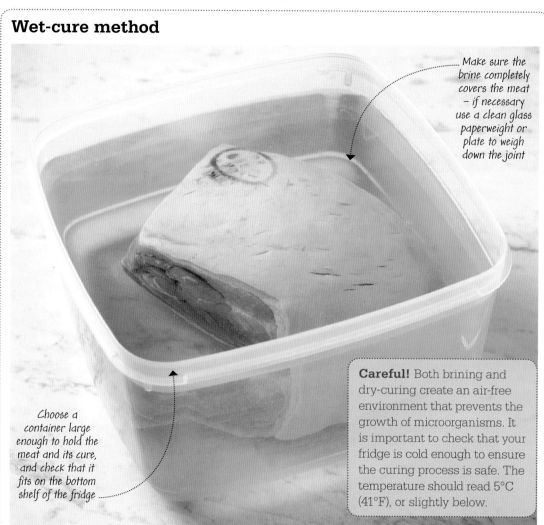

Make sure the brine completely covers the meat – if necessary use a clean glass paperweight or plate to weigh down the joint

Choose a container large enough to hold the meat and its cure, and check that it fits on the bottom shelf of the fridge

Careful! Both brining and dry-curing create an air-free environment that prevents the growth of microorganisms. It is important to check that your fridge is cold enough to ensure the curing process is safe. The temperature should read 5°C (41°F), or slightly below.

THE BRINING PROCESS

To cure, the raw meat must sit in a salty solution – sometimes for up to 25 days. Use a plastic container with an airtight lid, and make sure that the meat will be submerged throughout the process. Put the lid on the box and place it in the fridge for the required time.

Dry-cure method

Cover the meat completely with the dry-cure mix, pressing it down as you work ....

APPLYING THE DRY-CURE MIX

Salting meat not only draws out moisture, but is also an opportunity to add flavour. To apply the dry-cure mix, place the meat skin-side down on a clean chopping board. Use your fingers to spread the cure evenly over the flesh and fat, rubbing it into all the crevices.

The dry-cure mix flavours the meat and draws out moisture

Spoon off the liquid and discard it ....

ALLOWING THE MEAT TO MATURE

Place the cured meat on a drip tray in a plastic container, seal with an airtight lid, and store in the fridge for the required length of time to cure properly and allow the flavours to mature. Check the meat regularly and drain off any watery liquid that collects under the tray.

Practise DRY-CURING MEAT

Dry-cured Bacon

Dry-curing is a simple process, and a popular starting
point for beginners. It's also a great way to prepare
delicious breakfast bacon. Use fresh, good-quality
pork to ensure the tastiest results.

2kg (4½lb)   **8–12 days**   **2–3 months**

Ingredients

2kg (4½lb) boneless loin of pork

For the dry-cure mix

80g (2¾oz) curing salt

40g (1½oz) soft light brown sugar

1 rounded tsp citric or ascorbic acid
(vitamin C powder)

Equipment

mixing bowl

chopping board

large plastic container with lid and
drip tray or rack in the base

spoon

sharp knife

kitchen paper

muslin

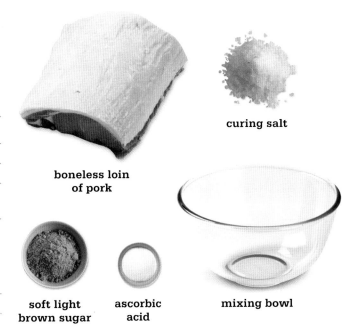

curing salt

boneless loin
of pork

soft light
brown sugar   ascorbic
acid   mixing bowl

chopping board

sharp knife

spoon

plastic container with drip tray

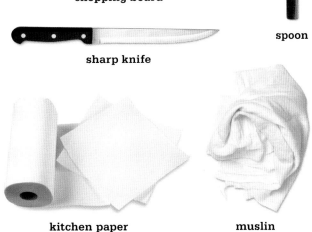

kitchen paper

muslin

1 Combine the ingredients for the dry-cure mix in a bowl. Lay the raw meat on a clean chopping board, skin-side down, and cover it with the cure mix.

Remember Always wash your hands before and after handling raw meat.

Rub the cure into all the exposed flesh including both ends

Don't forget to rub some of the curing mix into the skin

2 Transfer the meat to a large plastic container with a drip tray in the base and an airtight lid. Seal the container and place it on the bottom shelf of the fridge for 4–5 days.

Careful! It is important to be fastidious about hygiene when dealing with raw pork. Do not allow any other food in the fridge to come into contact with it.

3 Check the joint at regular intervals and drain off the watery liquid that collects below the drip tray. Rub any salty sediment back into the meat.

Why? If you allow the joint to reabsorb the curing juices, it will take longer for the meat to dry at the end of the process.

Use a spoon to drain the liquid

A uniformly pink colour indicates that the cure has reached the centre of the joint......

4 To check that the bacon is sufficiently cured, cut a thin slice from one end. It should be pink across the length of the slice.

Help! If you see a grey patch in the centre of the slice, make up half quantities of the curing mix and reapply to the joint. Put the meat back into the container, seal, and return it to the fridge for another 24 hours.

5 Rinse the joint in cold water and dry with kitchen paper. Wrap in clean muslin, place back in its container, and refrigerate uncovered – well away from other food – for another 4–5 days.

Why? Leaving the bacon in the fridge uncovered allows it to dry out a little more. The meat will darken and become firmer to the touch. Check it's ready to eat by frying and tasting a sample slice.

The drip tray helps air circulate during the drying process......

How to store

Wrap the bacon in greaseproof paper and store in the fridge for up to 10 days, cutting off slices as and when required. Though cured, the meat cannot be eaten raw and must be cooked.

Alternatively, divide the joint into conveniently-sized portions and freeze for 2–3 months.

Did anything go wrong?

The bacon tastes too salty after curing. Soak the joint in cold water in the fridge for 24 hours. Pat dry with kitchen paper and wrap in muslin. Refrigerate uncovered for another 3–4 days.

The meat has gone mouldy. If there is green or black mould on the cured meat, the storage atmosphere may have been too damp and warm. Discard the meat; do not eat.

Try more meat preserves ▶ ▶ ▶

Wet-cured Ham

There are many ways to cure pork into ham, but this basic method gives the meat a mild, sweet flavour. The sugar is an important ingredient in the cure mix as it helps to soften the meat, which might otherwise become toughened by the high salt content.

| 2.5kg (5½ lb) | 1 month | 4–5 days, cooked |

Ingredients

2.5kg (5½lb) horseshoe-cut
   of pork with skin on

For the cure mix

700g (1lb 9oz) curing salt

30g (1oz) light brown soft sugar

25g (scant 1oz) ascorbic acid
   (vitamin C powder)

For cooking and finishing the ham

2 small glasses cider

1 dried bay leaf

12 black peppercorns

6 cloves

Equipment

large plastic container with lid and drip
   tray or rack in the base

drip tray or rack

baking tray

kitchen string

muslin

large saucepan

**horseshoe-cut
of pork with
skin on**

**curing
salt**

**soft light
brown sugar**

**black
peppercorns**

**ascorbic
acid**

bay leaf

cloves

cider

**plastic container
with drip tray**

**kitchen
string**

baking tray

muslin

large saucepan

1 Put 6 litres (12½ pints) of water in a large sterilized plastic container with a lid. Add all the curing ingredients and stir the solution well until everything has dissolved.

Help! The cure will fizz and may smoke a little – don't worry, this is perfectly normal.

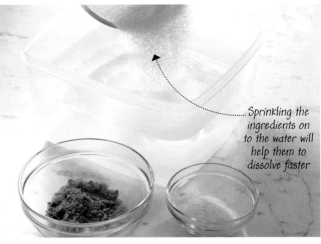

Sprinkling the ingredients on to the water will help them to dissolve faster

Check that the cure ingredients are fully dissolved before adding the pork joint

2 Place the meat in the container and make sure that it is completely submerged in the brine. Seal the container and refrigerate the pork for 25 days.

Tip If necessary use a clean plate or paperweight to weigh down the pork. Check regularly to ensure that the meat remains submerged throughout the curing time.

3 Lift the meat out of the brine and pat dry with kitchen paper. Place it on a rack or drip tray set over a baking tray, truss into a round with kitchen string, wrap the joint in muslin and refrigerate for 3–4 days.

Why? The drip tray will catch the moisture dripping from the pork as it dries out, and also allows air to circulate.

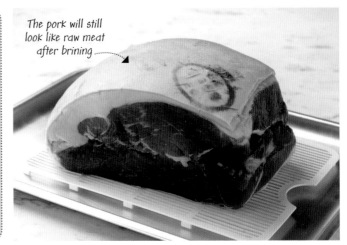

The pork will still look like raw meat after brining

4 To cook, soak the ham in cold water for 1 hour. Bring a large saucepan of water to the boil, add the cider, seasonings and ham, then bring back to the boil. Cover and barely simmer over gentle heat for 3–3½ hours.

Remember The ham is not ready to eat until it has been properly cooked.

The aromatic spices and cider enhance the flavour of the ham as it cooks

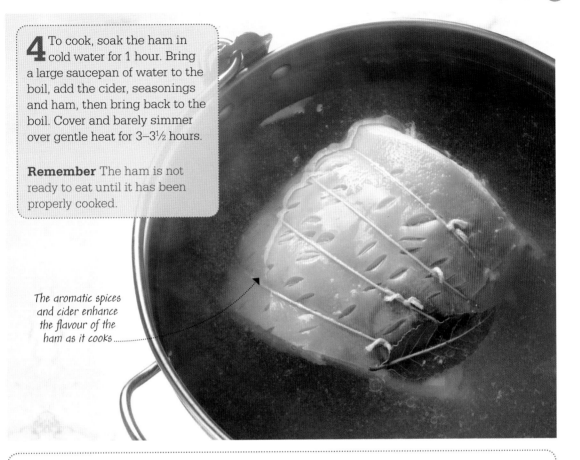

How to store

Boiled ham may be stored in the fridge for 4–5 days. Alternatively, divide into convenient portions and freeze for 2–3 months.

Honey roast ham is finished in the oven with a sweet glaze: mix 2 level tablespoons each of maple syrup, honey, and mustard, or use 5 tablespoons of marmalade. Spread the glaze over the ham. Roast in a hot oven (200°C/400°F/Gas 6) for 30–40 minutes. Cold roast ham keeps in the fridge for up to 5 days.

Uncooked cured meat may be refrigerated for up to 3 days, or frozen for 1–2 months.

Did anything go wrong?

The joint smells unpleasant. Discard the meat; do not eat it.

The brine has changed consistency. The curing mix didn't contain enough salt, or the storage temperature was too high. Re-do the whole process.

White salt burns appear on the cured meat. The salt solution was too strong.

The cured meat has green or black mould. Your salt solution was too weak, and the meat wasn't cured properly. Discard the meat.

Try more meat preserves ▶ ▶ ▶

How to **Pot Meats**

Succulent potted meats make delicious cheap and cheerful snacks – simply serve with toast. Potting is a great way to preserve cheap cuts, such as shin of beef or pork belly, and using this technique you can extend the life of leftovers too. Shred the cooked meat (or process to a paste), pot it, then seal with an airtight layer of clarified butter or lard.

Pack the meat

Cook the meat until tender and almost falling apart; reserve the juices. Blitz the meat in a food processor to make a smooth paste, or shred by hand for a more coarse-textured preserve. Allow it to cool, then pack into a warm sterilized jar, add any reserved juices, and level the top.

Leave at least 1cm (½in) for the layer of fat and firmly press in the meat

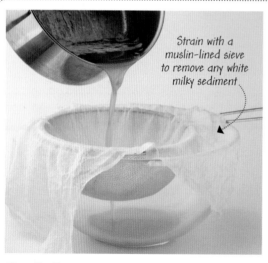

Strain with a muslin-lined sieve to remove any white milky sediment

The butter cools into a 1cm (½in) solid layer, blocking off bacteria

Seal the pot

A layer of fat creates an airtight seal that excludes airborne microbes but keeps the meat moist. Clarified butter (from which water and milk solids are removed) has a good shelf life, preserving the meat longer. Melt the butter in a pan over a low heat. Let it foam for a few seconds then remove from the heat, skim off the froth, and allow to cool slightly. Strain the melted butter into a bowl. Pour over the surface of the meat.

Potted Beef

Approx. 500g (1lb 2oz)

5–5½ hours

1 month refrigerated

Ingredients

900g (2lb) shin of beef, diced and trimmed of any fat

600ml (1 pint) beef stock

300ml (10fl oz) red wine

1 small onion, peeled and quartered

2 garlic cloves, peeled

few fresh bay leaves

few sprigs of thyme

pinch of ground mace

½ tsp mustard powder

350g (12oz) unsalted butter, softened

salt and freshly ground black pepper

Special Equipment

large casserole dish

food processor

muslin

ramekins or small serving dishes

Preheat the oven to 160°C (325°F/Gas 3).

COOK THE BEEF

Place the beef in a large casserole dish, pour over the stock and red wine, and scatter over the onion, garlic, bay leaves, and thyme. Bring to a simmer and then cover and cook in the oven for 2½–3 hours, until very tender.

Tip If you prefer, you can simmer the beef on a hob for the same length of time until tender.

CHOP THE MEAT

Drain the liquid and remove the onion, garlic, and herbs. Transfer the cooked meat to a food processor, add the mace, mustard, and 115g (4oz) of the softened butter, and process, or chop by hand if preferred, until smooth or slightly textured.

POT THE BEEF

Season the meat mixture liberally. Spoon the mixture into ramekins or small serving dishes and chill for 2 hours.

SEAL THE BEEF

Melt the remaining butter in a saucepan, skim off the scum and cool slightly. Pour the melted butter through a muslin-lined sieve, discarding the milky sediment leftat the bottom of the pan, and cool slightly.

Pour the clarified butter over the tops of the dishes to form a layer about 1cm (½in) thick. Chill until the butter has set, then garnish with bay leaves and cranberries if you like.

Pork Rillettes

1 small jar   **2 days**   **1 month, refrigerated**

Ingredients

1 tbsp rosemary, chopped

1 large garlic clove, crushed

¼ tsp cloves, ground

2 tsp sea salt

black pepper, freshly ground

500g (1lb 2oz) piece of fatty belly pork, on the bone

1 bay leaf

60g (2oz) lard, if needed

Special Equipment

small bowl

large plastic container with lid

casserole dish

foil

small saucepan

chopping board

small preserving jar

MAKE THE RUB

In a small bowl, mix together the rosemary, garlic, cloves, salt, and black pepper. Place the meat in a large container with a sealable lid and, using your hands, cover it in the rub.

Tip Cover the meat completely in the rub, using your fingers to work it thoroughly into the skin and meat.

Seal the container and store the meat in the fridge for 24 hours.

COOK THE MEAT

Preheat the oven to 150°C (300°F/Gas 2).

Transfer the meat to a casserole dish, and add the bay leaf and 250ml (8fl oz) boiling water. Cover the dish tightly with cooking foil, put the lid on, and cook in the low oven for 3 hours until the meat is really tender and almost falls off the bone.

Careful! The meat needs to stay moist as it cooks, so check it after 1½ hours of cooking time. If the water has evaporated, add a little more water – a couple of tablespoonfuls should be enough.

Take the casserole out of the oven and drain off and reserve the melted fat, which will have collected in a layer above the juices. Tip the pork and its juices into a sieve set over a bowl, cover, and allow to cool. If there is lots of fat in the juices, spoon it off and add it to the reserved fat. Reserve the juices too.

PACK THE JAR

Once the pork is cold, remove the rind and bones and discard them, and put the pork on a chopping board.

Shred the meat – use two forks back to back to pull it apart – and pack it into a sterilized jar. Add the reserved juices.

In a small saucepan, melt the reserved fat over a low heat. Pour it over the meat so that it covers the meat completely.

Tip If there isn't enough fat to cover the surface, melt some lard and add that to the jar.

Seal the jar, label, and, once cooled, refrigerate for up to 1 month.

Remember The pork rillettes keep for up to 2 days in the fridge after the jar is opened.

Duck Confit

4 servings **2¾ hours** **2 weeks, refrigerated**

Ingredients

2 tbsp sea salt

8 black peppercorns, lightly crushed

2 large garlic cloves, crushed

¼ tsp allspice, ground

1 tsp dried thyme

2 bay leaves, torn into pieces

4 portions duck leg

350g (12oz) goose or duck fat

a little lard, if needed

Special Equipment

small bowl

large plastic container with lid

medium casserole dish

frying pan (to reheat for serving)

MAKE THE RUB

In a small bowl, combine the salt, peppercorns, garlic, allspice, thyme, and bay leaves. Place the duck legs in a large container with a sealable lid and, using your hands, cover them in the rub.

Seal the container and store the duck legs in the fridge for 24 hours.

COOK THE MEAT

Preheat the oven to 150°C (300°F/Gas 2).

Rinse the duck legs thoroughly with cold water and pat dry with kitchen paper.

Why? Rinsing is important to prevent the finished dish tasting too salty – but the flavours from the rub are retained by the flesh.

Place the duck in a medium-sized flameproof casserole dish. Add the goose or duck fat and heat over a low heat until the fat has melted – for about 10 minutes.

Cover the dish with a lid and cook in the low oven for 2½ hours until the meat is really tender.

Take the meat out of the oven and set aside until fairly cool. Transfer to a container with a sealable lid and pour the fat over the top to cover the meat completely; if necessary add the extra lard. Seal, allow to cool, and store in the fridge.

SERVING THE CONFIT

Remove the duck from the container and scrape off the fat.

Tip Reserve the fat for the future: you can store it in the fridge and use it again for making confit up to 3 times.

Heat a large, heavy-based frying pan and fry the duck for about 5 minutes on each side. Fry the duck skin-side down, first over a high heat, then reduce the heat, turn the duck over, and cook until piping hot all the way through.

Index

Acknowledgements

Photographic Credits

Dorling Kindersley would like to thank **Peter Anderson** and **Dave King** for new photography.
All images © Dorling Kindersley.
For further information see
www.dkimages.com

Publisher's Acknowledgements

Many people helped in the making of this book.
Dorling Kindersley would like to thank:

In the UK

Design assistance Vicky Read
Editorial assistance Annelise Evans, Helen Fewster,
Holly Kyte
DK Images Claire Bowers, Freddie Marriage, Emma Shepherd,
Romaine Werblow
Indexer Chris Bernstein

In India

Senior Editor Garima Sharma
Senior Art Editor Ivy Roy
Design assistance Devan Das, Prashant Kumar, Ankita
Mukherjee, Anamica Roy, Suzena Sengupta
Editors Arani Sinha
Editorial assistance Suefa Lee, Swati Mittal
DTP Designers Rajesh Singh Adhikari, Sourabh Chhallaria,
Arjinder Singh
CTS/DTP Manager Sunil Sharma